CAN YOU FIND GOD IN NATURE AND STILL BE JEWISH?

"In the Hebrew Bible, wilder[ness] Torah is given, where D[avid] find inspiration, where Elija[h] voice' (1 Kings 19:12). Wild [is the] home of revelation.... It rema[ins a special], unique setting to meet God. For today's spiritual seekers, it is a place of potential and promise."

—from Chapter 1, "The Call of the Wild"

Judaism emerged from the Jewish people's experience in the desert. Is this coincidental, or is there an organic, vital connection between spirituality and wilderness?

Offering profound insights on the natural world's place in Jewish culture, this spiritual primer explores the partnership between wilderness and Judaism that began at Sinai. Traditional rituals and innovative practices will help Jews of any level of nature experience to engage with the wilderness in ways that enrich Jewish spiritual life—and help establish a direct relationship with God.

Rabbi Mike Comins, the founder of TorahTrek Spiritual Wilderness Adventures (www.TorahTrek.com) and the Institute for Jewish Wilderness Spirituality (www.ijws-online.org), is the author of *Making Prayer Real: Leading Jewish Spiritual Voices on Why Prayer Is Difficult and What to Do about It* (Jewish Lights). He studied classical Jewish texts at the Pardes Institute, earned his MA in Jewish education from Hebrew University and was ordained in the Israeli rabbinical program of Hebrew Union College. He was a founding member and the first director of education at Kehilat Kol Haneshama in Jerusalem. He lives, teaches and writes in Los Angeles, and serves as a scholar-in-residence for schools and synagogues around the world.

Nigel Savage founded and runs Hazon (www.hazon.org).

A Wild FAITH

Jewish Ways into Wilderness, Wilderness Ways into Judaism

Rabbi Mike Comins

Foreword by Nigel Savage

JEWISH LIGHTS Publishing

FOR MY PARENTS

A Wild Faith:
Jewish Ways into Wilderness, Wilderness Ways into Judaism

2014 Second Printing

For information regarding permission to reprint material from this book, please mail or fax your request in writing to Jewish Lights Publishing, Permissions Department, at the address / fax number listed below, or email your request to permissions@jewishlights.com.

I am extremely grateful to Joseph Cornell and Dawn Publications of Nevada City, California, for permission to use exercises found in *Sharing Nature with Children, Twentieth Anniversary Edition* and *Sharing Nature with Children II.* Excerpts from *Listening to Nature* by Joseph Cornell. Copyright ©1987 by Joseph Cornell. Reprinted by permission of Dawn Publications. Excerpts from *God in Search of Man* by Abraham Joshua Heschel. Copyright © 1955 by Abraham Joshua Heschel. Copyright renewed 1983 by Sylvia Heschel. Reprinted by permission of Farrar, Straus and Giroux, LLC.

© 2007 by Michael Comins

Library of Congress Cataloging-in-Publication Data
Comins, Mike.
A wild faith : Jewish ways into wilderness, wilderness ways into Judaism / Mike Comins.
p. cm.
Includes bibliographical references and index.
ISBN: 978-1-58023-316-3 (pbk.)
ISBN: 978-1-68162-968-1 (hc.)
1. Spiritual life—Judaism. 2. Nature—Religious aspects—Judaism. 3. Hiking. 4. Meditation—Judaism. I. Title.
BM723.C65 2007
296.7—dc22

2007001134

ISBN 978-1-58023-589-1 (eBook)

Cover design: Tim Holtz

Manufactured in the United States of America

Published by Jewish Lights Publishing
www.jewishlights.com

CONTENTS

Contents

ACKNOWLEDGMENTS

I shared several ideas for a book with freelance editor Donna Zerner after she participated in a *Torah Trek* retreat. She politely told me to put them on a shelf and, instead, write a primer on Jewish spiritual practice in wilderness. I followed her advice, but when I sent her my first book proposal, most of it ended up in the circular file. I went back to the drawing board. The second proposal was entitled *A Wild Faith*. This book would not have been written without her wise counsel.

My thanks to Stuart Matlins and the Jewish Lights staff, particularly Maura Shaw, for discovering me a few weeks before I submitted that proposal, and Emily Wichland, for patiently and kindly shepherding this first-time author through the maze of writing a book. My editor, Bryna Fischer, improved the manuscript immensely through her insightful criticism on issues of both content and style. Her knowledge, creativity, and patience are greatly appreciated.

A number of friends generously donated their time and expertise in reading drafts of the manuscript. Many thanks to Rickey Berkowitz, Claire Gorfinkel, Mary Hoffman, Jody Porter, Rabbi David Seidenberg, Jenna Snow, and Darcy Vebber. I also received the help of rabbis Jill Hammer and Gershon Winkler.

I have enjoyed an eclectic education in a multitude of educational centers and organizations, and all of their voices come through in this book. My heartfelt thanks to Hebrew Union

College, Jerusalem; the Pardes Institute of Jewish Studies, Jerusalem; Hebrew University; the Israel Ministry of Tourism (for their desert guide course); the Elat Chayyim Center for Jewish Spirituality; Metivta, A Center for Contemplative Judaism; The Institute for Jewish Spirituality; the Spirit Rock Meditation Center; Sacred Passage; and C-Deep.

I have learned from too many superb teachers to list here. Nevertheless, at the risk of offending, I am compelled to mention those whose spiritual teachings directly contributed to this book: David Abram, Sylvia Boorstein, Rabbi Shefa Gold, Dr. Arthur Green, Israel Hevroni, Jack Kornfield, Rabbi Chaim Meiersdorf, John Milton, John Travis, Rabbi Gershon Winkler; and those who taught me through their writings and work: Ellen Bernstein, Dr. Eugene Borowitz, Rabbi David Cooper, Joseph Cornell, and Rabbi Lawrence Kushner.

Thanks to all who have supported *Torah Trek:* those who participated in a *Torah Trek* program; the organizations and institutions who commissioned *Torah Trek* programs; and the wonderful folks of the Jewish Community of Jackson Hole, who brought me to Wyoming and gave me a job in wilderness paradise. Thank you, Mitch Dann.

Special thanks to Marty (Martha) Peale.

Outdoor Jewish education and adventure programming is a lonely endeavor. I have gained strength and inspiration from my friends and colleagues who, against all odds, have pursued their passion in wilderness: Rabbi Howard Cohen (Burning Bush Adventures), Dr. Gabe Goldman (currently at the Brandeis-Bardin Institute), Rabbi Jamie Korngold (Adventure Rabbi), and Josh Lake (Outdoor Jewish Adventures). I have also been blessed with the friendship of fellow traveler and confidant on the path to spiritual practice, Rabbi Helen Cohn.

My gratitude as well to the beautiful place, people, and programs of the Murie Center in Jackson Hole, Wyoming.

Many thanks to the friendly folks at my "office," the crew at the Platt Avenue Starbucks in West Hills, California.

If you want to torture your partner and strain a relationship, try writing a book. My amazing partner has never complained. Thanks to Jody, for her patience, back rubs, and endless love.

My earliest memories are of places in wilderness, as my parents took me camping before I could speak. I was graced to spend my childhood summers in Big Sur and Yosemite. When the RV revolution hit and the campgrounds suddenly became crowded and noisy, my parents took the revolutionary decision (at least in their circles) to outfit the family with down jackets and sleeping bags. I was twelve, my sister, Felicia, nine, and my brother, Alan, six when the family started backpacking. I'm sure they had no idea what they were starting in the life of their son.

My father, Harold, has blessed me with his analytical mind; my mother, Dorothy, has blessed me with her artist's heart. Both have given me the gift of wilderness. It has not been easy for my parents to watch their son forsake a normal career path to follow his dreams, first to Israel, then to wilderness. But they have done so with love and understanding, and I could not have done it without their steadfast support. This book is not only a writing project. It is the product of a life's journey, and I hope my parents see themselves in it as much as they see me. With love, I dedicate this book to them.

A NOTE ON THE TEXT

Unless otherwise noted, biblical quotes are from the New JPS Translation—Second Edition in the *JPS Hebrew-English Tanakh* (Philadelphia: Jewish Publication Society, 1999). In the interests of presenting gender-neutral language vis-à-vis a gender-neutral Being, "Adonai" has been substituted for the usual English translation of LORD.

Were they alive in our time, Abraham Joshua Heschel and Martin Buber would most likely have written in gender-neutral language. However, to present their quotes accurately, their words have not been altered. Hopefully, this will not be a barrier between readers and these two gifted teachers.

FOREWORD

There are two sorts of people who should be reading this book: The first are those who have not spent much (or perhaps any) time in the wilderness; the second are those who have spent *lots* of time in the wilderness. I imagine that I was invited to write this Foreword because I used to be in the first group and now I am in the second.

I had two key moments of transition from the first group to the second, and the initial one was not in wilderness at all: it was in Golders Hill Park in North West London, on a cold clear early February morning. I was walking through the park and reading an affirmation from *Life! Reflections on Your Journey* by Louise Hay. The words were: "I listen to the divine, and rejoice at all that I can hear." And as I walked through the park, and said these words, and looked at the trees, and felt the cold, and saw the ducks on the lake, I felt my relationship with the world around me change. It was some years after this that I first read Jewish theologian Abraham Joshua Heschel and came upon his idea of experiencing radical amazement when in the presence of the Divine; and when I did so, I understood that my first sense of radical amazement had been that morning in the park.

The second moment of transition was in November 1994. A friend of mine invited me to join him and three other men in hiking "from sea to sea"—in this case, from the Mediterranean Sea to the Sea of Galilee. I agreed without much thought. Six weeks later I was standing at the foot of the *midrachov* (pedestrian mall) in the center of Jerusalem, in drizzling rain, wearing what seemed like an eighty-pound pack on my back, saying to myself: *Nige! You've made a dreadful mistake!* I didn't think I'd last twenty minutes carrying that pack, much less four days.

But four nights later, at the end of the hike, I stumbled into Lake Kinneret, exhausted and exhilarated. We'd chosen to hike on Shabbat (the only time when I have done so) and it was time for *Havdalah.* We dropped our packs on the shore, stripped off our clothes, and waded into the water. We carried with us a *Havdalah* candle, an overflowing cup of wine, and a fragrant overripe pineapple we'd picked up just yards from the shore. In the darkness of the water, with a multitude of stars above, and with the lights of Tiberias twinkling down the lake, together we sang the ancient blessings that mark the end of Shabbat and the start of the week.

Even though I had made *Havdalah* countless times before in my life, this was a different *Havdalah,* just as davenning had been different during the hike. The Jewish people didn't arise in a synagogue or temple; our prayer life didn't develop in a suburban building; the words of our prayers and of the psalms did not begin with a siddur. The beauty and rhythm and wisdom of Jewish tradition arose in an encounter with the majesty and awe of the physical world around us. Something about being outdoors, being exposed, being physically challenged, being bereft of electrical toys and the protection of metal and brick and glass, being in contact with the wind and trees and animals—all this had a profound impact on me.

These two experiences capture so much of what is central and vital in *A Wild Faith.* One can walk through a park any day. It was only because of my particular consciousness—because of a particular set of words that I was saying, with intention—that my actual experience of the physical world changed. It was because I pushed myself in Israel that I learned the value of being exposed, and discovered that I was so much stronger and more capable than I realized. It is because we seem to have forgotten these things that this book is so important and so necessary. There is a generation of Jews steadily engaging with the physical world and there are others who are reaccessing the tradition in many ways, but too often these disparate elements of our development remain unconnected. Jewish tradition is ancient and wise, and it comes alive in the world around us—with the help of a guide like Rabbi Comins, at once learned and searching, honest and thoughtful, rooted and open.

This work is not just personally enriching, it is also important. The organization that I founded and run, Hazon, works to create a healthier and more sustainable Jewish community—as a step toward a healthier and more sustainable world for all. It has become abundantly clear these last few years that our way of life is straining the planet's ability to support us. We're destroying ecosystems, damaging the topsoil, polluting air and water and, perhaps above all, undertaking a dangerous and uncontrolled experiment in climate change. These interlinked challenges seem overwhelming, and in many ways they are. But the heart of our response must derive from two sources. The first is a sense of reconnection with the physical world. We have to fall in love, or refall in love, with this amazing world that sustains us. We protect what we know, and know what we love. Hiking and biking and davenning in the world's open spaces, and doing so with thought and awareness, is a vital first step in transforming how we experience the world—and how we treat it.

The second thing we need to do is to reaccess ancient wisdom in new ways. This book steadily bears the imprint of learning from other traditions—Buddhism, Daoism, Christianity, Native American. But the obverse of this is the extent to which Jewish tradition is itself one of the world's most ancient resources. Celebrating Shabbat as a day of rest; respecting *shmitta* (respite for the land every seventh year); understanding *brachot* (blessings) as a mindfulness practice; seeing halakhah itself as a way of treasuring the importance and possibility of voluntary self-restraint; all these traditional Jewish ideas come alive in the twenty-first century when we see them through the new eyes of global citizens. I hope that this book will be read not only by thoughtful Jews, but also by people of other faiths, and of none, who care to learn and grow.

The world is a complicated place. It's not easy to live healthily or sustainably. Yet I have slowly learned not merely that it's possible, but that the heart of transformation is about openness, joy, celebration, listening, learning, and being present. This book is wise and beautiful. I bless you, and me, and all of us, that we learn to live more generously, walk more lightly, and feel more deeply, on this our beautiful world.

Nigel Savage

1

THE CALL
OF THE WILD

In all of ancient Near Eastern literature, the Bible is one
of the few texts that knows wilderness as a place of
majesty, a place where God lets himself be known....
Far from rejecting nature, the Hebrews embrace her as
a whole, thorns and all.

Evan Eisenberg[1]

The Jewish New Year, Rosh Hashanah, September 1996: I am
camped snugly against the cliffs of a canyon in the desert mountains above the Israeli city of Eilat. The vertical walls rise a hundred feet toward the stars. The soft limestone, streaked with
yellows and oranges that mirror the sunrise, envelops me. In this
private cathedral I am protected, though the stark, dry riverbed
leaves me a bit unsettled. I wrap myself in my *tallit*, my prayer
shawl, against the early morning cold in that brief moment when
shade is the enemy, and listen to the birds for inspiration. I begin
to sing the ancient words of praise to the Creator of this sacred
place. Memories enter my awareness: backpacking in Sequoia
with my family, watching the sunrise from Mount Sinai with
friends in college. I recite a psalm and speak words of yearning
to God.

It is time to welcome the New Year as Jews have done over the millennia. It is, in the tradition, the Day of Judgment, where all stand before the Holy One, accountable for their deeds in the previous year. Like the acacia trees and salt plants beside me, I am fully exposed. Far from humans, in God's handiwork, my heart sheds its burdens and my prayers flow.

It was a superb Rosh Hashanah. The words I spoke to God were sincere and true, emotionally charged with yearning, infused with awe and love. By every measure, this was what the architects of Jewish ritual had in mind—except for one thing. I wasn't in synagogue. I didn't pray in the required minyan of ten. And at that time, this was a particularly sensitive point. I had been ordained just two months earlier. My first Rosh Hashanah as a rabbi was my first Rosh Hashanah away from the Jewish community in two decades. What would my teachers think of me now?

As the sun rose and the shade receded, I thought about the long and circuitous road to this desert canyon. I had spent the previous three years working feverishly on a rabbinic thesis devoted to theology. I was constantly thinking about God, but as the months went by I felt further and further away from the kind of spiritual experience that led me to writing the thesis in the first place. I davened, or prayed, in one of the best places on earth to daven, Kehilat Kol HaNeshamah in Jerusalem. But after ten years, my devotion was waning and my prayer life had become stale. When I finished my thesis, I felt compelled to do something for my heart that I had neglected for years. I went hiking.

Walking a trail is second nature to me. My parents never missed a summer visit to Yosemite. I grew up backpacking in the "Range of Light," the incredible Sierra Nevada mountains of California. But as I lived an observant, traditional life in Jerusalem, I spent the one Israeli day off, Shabbat, in synagogue. Now, feeling suffocated from books and buildings, I returned to the source of my first spiritual feelings, to wilderness. It was like jumping into an alpine lake, a wake-up call that soothes the spirit by shocking the system.

I walked the deserts, the only true wilderness in Israel. I went to stop thinking about theology. So what happened caught me by surprise.

God kicked in.

Before then I had been a wannabe when it came to God. I wanted to experience God in my life. And I tried. I went to Orthodox yeshiva and liberal rabbinical school. I lived the pious Jerusalem life. Now I know what I failed to admit to myself then: a personal relationship with God was missing. I rarely allowed myself to think about it. After all, Jewish religious life is so communal that one need not worry if an individual experience of God is lacking. There is no requirement for a Jew to compose his or her own words of prayer or listen for God in silence. Jewish communal religiosity can be so powerful, soulful, and moving, one can make do quite nicely without feeling a lack of spiritual passion. But now the communal experience no longer satisfied. I needed more.

I turned to the desert. Between hikes, I read what I felt like reading for the first time in years. I was exposed to nonacademic works on Jewish mysticism (thank you, Rabbi Lawrence Kushner), to Eastern mystics and the Desert Fathers (early Christian monks who settled the same desert locale). Suddenly I had a theory, an understanding that helped open me to God in wilderness. Suddenly I had a language to articulate what I had always felt in wilderness but could not connect to Judaism or the Jewish community. I began to feel something that I believe must be similar to what the psalmist felt before writing the psalm. I was feeling God in my bones. I began to trust my intuition. I stopped talking and began to listen. Instead of thinking, I walked. Instead of looking from my brain, I followed my body.

I had plans to continue on for a PhD, but there was no going back. My life had changed. Instead of Hebrew University, I went to Sde Boker in Israel's great desert, the Negev, and qualified as an Israeli desert guide. I began leading spiritual desert trips in the Judean desert and the Sinai, filled mostly with rabbis, rabbinic students, and students for the ministry. I found myself on the journey that led to the writing of this book.

So I left the synagogue that Rosh Hashanah. It was an act filled with irony. I would not have felt the need to spend Rosh Hashanah in a place where God was so present to me if Jewish culture had not taught me that God exists and is available to human beings. Yet, to gain that experience, I felt compelled to rebel against the very tradition that planted the thirst for God within me!

NATURE OR TORAH?

Putting away my *tallit*, I paused to look at the prayer book in my hands, and then the orange limestone under the bright blue sky. I thought about the great debate that has occupied Jewish thinkers over the millennia. It has resurfaced with great intensity due to the environmental crisis and the fact that large numbers of Jews are hiking, skiing, kayaking, and climbing in wilderness. Where do we find God? From where does revelation come? Wilderness or the Book? Nature or Torah?

Obviously, the answer can be both. After all, the Torah was given in wilderness! But now that we have Torah and its always evolving commentary, do we find God in printed words, through reading learned texts and praying the inherited words of the prayer book? Or do we find God at the original site of revelation, in the natural world, without words at all?

Of course, the preferred answer would be both. But, in fact, it rarely happens that way. Entering wilderness to experience God's presence is not a concept taken seriously by the major institutions of Jewish life in America and elsewhere. Jewish spiritual training centers on intellectual acumen and study, study, study! I spent twelve hours a day at the yeshiva. Rabbinical school put me in a library, not on a trail. The deserts of David, Amos, and Jeremiah were just down the road, but we went there to get a break from our studies, not to further the spiritual quest.

One need not look to Jewish cultural history to know this Torah/nature conflict. I stand on a ridge overlooking the Sinai wilderness with the siddur, the Jewish prayer book, in hand. Do I recite a psalm praising the Creator for the grandeur of nature, or do I just look up? And if, in fact, I feel closer to God when I look away from the book, why do I need the siddur at all? But what would happen to the People of the Book if books, the vehicles of Jewish tradition, were secondary to what we experience firsthand?

My personal dilemma is, in fact, played out daily in the life of the Jewish people. As one who frequents backcountry trails as well as mainstream Jewish communal institutions, I have learned: most Jews who love wilderness know little of Judaism, and most committed Jews know little of wilderness.

THE TORAH/NATURE DIVIDE

Every author has a reader in mind when writing. *A Wild Faith* could have been written for those on one side of the Torah/nature divide, but it is intended for both.

The first reader, let's call him Wilderness Jew, feels intensely alive in the natural world. He doesn't consider himself a religious person. Hebrew school was an ordeal to be overcome and left behind after bar mitzvah. The idea of a punishing and rewarding God in heaven makes little sense. What's left of his Jewish identity may have more to do with bagels than the Bible.

But he recognizes the importance of some kind of spirituality in his life. And in the beauty, the strong emotions, and the exhilarating excitement of the natural world, he unquestionably knows that there is something profound and moving in wilderness. He senses the natural world as meaningful for its own sake, ethically commanding, and sacred—in short, holy.

On the other end of the spectrum we find Religious Jew. In this person's self-understanding, Jewish identity is prominent. She celebrates Jewish holidays, gives *tzedakah* (charity), socializes in the Jewish community. She may even pray three times a day. God-language is not a problem. But like all regular worshipers, she knows that the connection to God is elusive and fickle, here today, gone tomorrow. It is all too easy for the prayers to become rote, devoid of the electricity generated by a living relationship with divinity.

And yet, right around the corner, there is a wilderness place in which most people say they feel something that can only be described as transcendent and sacred. In Religious Jew's education, little if any connection has been made between this experience and her self-understanding as a Jew. Yet she knows what she feels. There is something special in the splendor of the natural world.

Religious Jew is moved because wilderness is a place where the "problem of God" is neither contrived nor irrelevant. In the struggle to keep one's ongoing religious practice fresh, wilderness is helpful because the felt presence of God is readily and reliably available. Religious Jew needs the natural world. *Wilderness matters because it is an optimal place to work out a personal, unscripted, fresh relationship with divinity.*

Wilderness Jew's situation is not to be envied, either. He struggles to find an acceptable vocabulary to express his most profound and noble emotions. He intuitively knows the moral implications of his feelings, but can't really explain why. He is missing a framework to integrate his feelings of awe and wonder into the larger ethical fabric of his life. And he lacks the means to take it home. Since his spirituality is alive in wilderness and absent in the city, when he leaves wilderness, he leaves his spiritual life behind. To my mind, Wilderness Jew has much to gain from Jewish observance. *Judaism matters because it offers a vocabulary and a practice to translate the sublime experience of wilderness into a life of purpose and meaning, a life lived in community, a life of beauty, integrity, and moral action.*

Thankfully, the Torah/nature divide is not set in stone. One need not choose between wilderness and Judaism.

In the course of this book, we shall see how wilderness leads to Judaism—to a deeper, more vibrant Jewish practice. The increased awareness required to travel safely in wilderness not only protects us, it also prepares us for the encounter with God. Many Jewish practices can be far more effective when practiced in wild nature. And many Jewish thinkers—medieval Jewish mystics, Hasidic rabbis, and modern thinkers like Martin Buber and Abraham Joshua Heschel—sought to renew Jewish life by explicating their experience of God in the natural world.

Conversely, Judaism leads us to wilderness—to absorb wilderness in deeper, more vibrant ways. Jewish practices help us to slow down and truly experience all that the natural world offers to our senses. Through blessings and prayer, we give expression to the intense emotions we feel in the incomparable beauty of nature. And as we give voice to our appreciation and gratitude for this incredible planet, our connection to the natural world grows in richness and strength. Finally, Judaism translates the experience of awe into moral meaning and ethical responsibility.

Wilderness Jew and Religious Jew are caricatures, of course. We are likely to find a bit of each in our hearts, and this is fitting. Wilderness and Judaism are joined at the hip.

In the Hebrew Bible, wilderness is where the Torah is given, where David and the psalmists find inspiration, where Elijah hears the "still, small voice" (1 Kings 19:12). Wilderness is the enduring home of revelation. Human culture has changed a great deal over the last four millennia. Thankfully, wilderness has not. What's left of it, anyway. It remains a special, unique setting to meet God. For today's spiritual seekers, it is a place of potential and promise.

THE CALL OF THE TIMES

In offering a primer on Jewish spiritual practice in wilderness, it is my hope that readers will come to understand that the organic partnership between wilderness and Judaism begun in Sinai over thirty-five hundred years ago is just as relevant now as it was then. In the age of global warming, when the quality of our grandchildren's world hangs in the balance, I believe that the renewal of our spiritual relationship with the natural world is the calling of our generation. For many Jews, that relationship will begin with the rediscovery of wilderness.

We need to unearth our wild roots.

THE STEREOTYPE OF THE "UNNATURAL" JEW

> Many of our ancestors took to the wilderness. Abraham, Jacob, and Moses were all called to forsake their settled lives, their homes, and their communities to endure a period of uncertainty and unfamiliarity in the desert. It was only in the unknown that true self-knowledge could be obtained. There they would meet God, discover their sense of purpose, and become Jews.
>
> Ellen Bernstein[1]

The response is inevitable. When I tell people that I lived and worked in Jackson Hole as a rabbi, eyebrows rise and jaws drop. "There are Jews in Wyoming?!"

Of course there are, and the number is growing. But plenty of other Jews can't entertain the thought. Never mind that some sixty meadows, lakes, and alpine peaks in the most remote area of California's Sierra Nevada mountains were named by the first man to travel them in modern times, Theodore Solomons, or that "the Bob," the million-acre wilderness area below Glacier National Park in Montana was named after the pioneering Jewish forester Bob

Marshall. In the minds of many, Jews just don't *do* that outdoor stuff.

As a rabbi who leads wilderness trips, people sometimes look at me like I'm a curious new type of comic book hero, with mysterious powers and an admirable if unfathomable mission. A reporter for a Jewish newspaper in Florida said to me in preparation for an interview, "You're going to have to explain this to me from the beginning. To me, roughing it is going from a hotel to a motel."

Television and the big screen, often in the hands of Jewish writers, seem to go out of their way to portray Jews as wilderness rejects. Hollywood, witness Woody Allen and now Ben Stiller, loves its Jewish men impish, wimpish, neurotic, and, of course, urban. Remember Billy Crystal as the Jewish dude in *City Slickers*. In *The Frisco Kid*, Gene Wilder plays a rabbi traveling though the Wild West like a fish out of water. It is his comic counterpoint, a rugged cowboy played by Harrison Ford, who can handle the great outdoors. That Ford himself is part Jewish, with a ranch in Jackson Hole, is no consolation.

The reality on the ground is quite different. I can testify that in areas adjacent to wilderness in Wyoming and Montana, the number of Jewish residents increases every year. The mountains are frequented by Jewish hikers, backpackers, skiers, and kayakers. So often I begin a conversation in English and finish it in Hebrew. Israelis love wilderness!

But the cultural image of the "unnatural Jew"[2] is troubling because it is often internalized by Jewish children who don't know better. Even among Jews at home in wilderness, the image persists. It's the American or Canadian or Israeli part of me that goes into the backcountry. When I do Jewish things, I'm in the city, under a roof. *A Wild Faith* is part of the growing effort by Jewish environmental educators to destroy this cultural stereotype.

THE NATURE OF JUDAISM

It is a difficult task. We have been taught that the Hebrew Bible is a record of the Israelites' battle against paganism, a worldview that locates divinity solely in the forces of nature. Different gods were in the sun, the moon, the storm, or the sea. The Israelites, on the other hand, perceived that God is beyond nature. Unlike the gods, who displayed the same immoral behavior as humans, transcendent God created the world and demands justice. The ancient Israelites discovered that God's arena is in historical events. Look for God in the Exodus and the revelation at Mount Sinai. Mountains and forests and flowers are for pagans.[3] No wonder we Wilderness Jews have trouble linking our perception of the natural world as sacred to Judaism and Torah.

There is truth in this mistaken interpretation of the Hebrew Bible. In the West, the ancient Israelites were indeed the first culture, as a culture, to recognize the divine nature of justice and apply it equitably to everyone. And God, of course, does manifest in historical events. For the Israelites, God is not limited to nature. But this account is seriously flawed. Not only has paganism been falsely caricaturized, but God's relation to the natural world in the eyes of the ancient Israelites has been thoroughly misrepresented.

In fact, Israelite religion focused mainly on the natural world. The reason was simple: the Israelites needed to eat. Unlike the irrigation farming of Egypt and Mesopotamia, Israelite agriculture depended on the timing and intensity of the rains. Drought and pestilence meant suffering and death. When Canaan suffered drought, the ancient Israelites left their homes for neighboring countries to avoid starvation, like Abraham and, later, Jacob's sons. The main goal of ancient Israelite religion was to ensure timely rains and productive soil.

In the Temple rituals, first fruits from the fields, orchards, and flocks were brought as sacrifices to the One who brought fertility to the seeds and rain to the soil. The three major pilgrimage holidays celebrated the three major harvests of Israelite agriculture—Pesach (Passover) for barley, Shavuot for wheat, and Sukkot for fruit. The one historical event marked was the Exodus from Egypt, with the banishment of leavened products over Pesach and dwelling in booths during Sukkot. Originally a separate observance, Pesach was apparently combined with the barley harvest, since both occurred in the spring. But no hierarchy is established.[4] The remembrance of the Exodus is not privileged over thanksgiving for the harvest, or vice versa. God in history is not extolled at the expense of God in nature.

In fact, the Hebrews were so grounded in the natural world, their experience of God was itself sensual. In contradiction to post-biblical theology (and its attempt to reinterpret scripture), an unbiased reading of the Torah shows that God is rarely revealed without a specific connection to nature. When Abraham calls out to God, he does so near majestic oak trees recognized as sacred shrines (Gen. 12:6, 13:18). Mountains are frequently sites of revelation, and not only Mount Sinai (Gen. 12:8, 22:14).

More astounding to our modern sensibilities, God appears in and through wild nature. God's presence is explicitly mediated by natural phenomena. God speaks to Job out of the "whirlwind," that is, a typical Mediterranean rainstorm. Fire is a preferred medium for the divine, as Moses discovers at the burning bush (Exod. 3:2). God appears to Abraham as fire and smoke (Gen. 15:17), and likewise to the Israelites during their forty-year desert sojourn (Exod. 13:21). God descends into the Tabernacle (Exod. 40:34–35), and later the Temple, as a cloud (1 Kings 8:10–11). And it is in fire and smoke that God descends for the greatest revelation of all on Mount Sinai (Exod. 19:18).

We, of course, have been taught that God is invisible. So it is incredible and ironic from the prejudices of our twenty-first-century worldview that when the Torah wants to emphasize God's overwhelming power and unique Otherness—transcending human understanding and independent of nature—God appears through exceptional but thoroughly natural phenomena.

The Torah records that it was dangerous to see God directly (Exod. 33:20). Only Moses does so—just once and only God's "back" (Exod. 33:23). On the other occasions, as mentioned above, God's presence is mediated. But the important point is this: Everyone knew that God appeared visibly in the world. God was tangible. In fact, as Yale Bible scholar James Kugel has demonstrated, God (and not angels) repeatedly takes human form in the Hebrew Bible.[5]

And that, I believe, explains why the fight against idolatry was so important. No one postulated a purely spiritual God beyond time and space that lives in some dimension other than the earth. (According to some biblical authors, God lived in the heavens, but that was part of this world, the place above the clouds next to the stars.) Because everyone agreed that God manifests primarily in the earth, it was imperative to understand the relationship between God and nature correctly.

Yes, God is in the mountain, but God transcends the mountain as well. Yes, God is in the fire, but God is more than fire or any other element.[6] Yes, God might appear as a human being, but at the same time, God is beyond human form.

Of course, our perceptions of God have changed in the last three thousand years. Not many of us are likely to explain the encounter with God as did our biblical ancestors. But the lesson for contemporary Jews is clear: Those who find God in nature have more in common with the creators of Judaism than those who do not. Israelite religion was indigenous—a direct response by the original settlers to the demands of their particular, local environment. Judaism was shaped by the Land of Israel.[7] The perception of God as transcendent and universal is consistent with God as tangible and immanent, dwelling in and working through the natural processes of the Israelite landscape. The natural world is not reserved for pagans; it is the most important arena for God's involvement with the world.[8]

Those of us who find God in nature in addition to history need not feel inauthentic as Jews. Jewishly speaking, to denigrate God's presence in the natural world would be, well, unnatural.

DO I HAVE TO BELIEVE IN GOD?

> What is the way that will lead to the proper love and fear of God? When you contemplate God's great, wondrous works and creatures, and from them obtain a glimpse of divine wisdom...
>
> **Maimonides[1]**

"But Rabbi, to be a Jew in wilderness, do I need to believe in God? I'm spiritual. I love nature. I feel those transcendent moments you speak about. But *God*? Organized religion? Please...."

"I understand," I reply. "In fact, I don't believe in God either...."

That's not exactly true, but I often start a class with just that statement nonetheless. I don't believe in God. Let me explain.

In America, "belief" is a term popularized by the general, Christian culture, and Christianity is a creed-based religion. Christians define themselves as people who confess to certain beliefs—the technical term is dogma—about God, Christ, and the afterlife. Hence the great importance of being a "believer."

Much of mainstream Christianity, across various denominations, understands that belief as illogical or against appearances or against common sense. Many identify with Soren

Kierkegaard. To believe in God requires a "leap" of faith "by virtue of the absurd."[2] The believer earns great merit for holding true what cannot be seen by the naked eye or proven by philosophy and science.

It's different, of course, for Jews. With the important exception of conversion, being a Jew is established by birth rather than one's theology. But more important, this line of spiritual thinking is hard to find in Judaism. So I cringe when well-intentioned Christian friends refer to me as a fellow believer in the community of faith. It's not that they're entirely wrong, but the process is usually different for Jews. "Faith" in Hebrew is *emunah*, which comes from the root for "trust." "Do you believe in God?" in Hebrew comes out, "Do you trust in God?" This is not alien to the English word "faith," but it's not the same either.

The question of trust presupposes the more basic question: Does God exist at all? For most of Jewish history, it did not occur to people to doubt God's existence. Today, it is a real question for most Jews.

"Belief" is usually an assertion of fact. I believe the sun will rise tomorrow. Scientific proofs can be brought for or against, though we will not know for sure until tomorrow morning. I would be happy if belief were used this way in theological conversations. But in America, religious "belief" is understood as true despite appearances or in opposition to what science can live with. So when people ask me, "Do you believe in God?" I reply, no. Rather, I *recognize* God. I perceive God's presence in the world.

This brings me to the first point I'd like to make to the Jewish atheist or agnostic. It's not about what you believe. It's about what you see—what you discern in the world and how you understand your experience.

Most of our lives can be described without reference to religion. We don't need God to talk about art, ethics, psychology, or politics. Of course, these fields can and do overlap with religion. Thus academics can study religious ethics, religious art, and so on. Followers of psychologist Carl Jung can understand God as the collective unconscious. But these fields need no religious language.

There is one set of terms, however, that is exclusive to religion: holy, sacred, sanctified, hallowed, blessed. If you use these words to describe parts of your experience in life, you are likely feeling the impulse that gives birth to religion. When we sense the sacredness of nature, we feel alive and energized, yet humble and connected to the world around us. The world is luminous. In philosopher Rudolf Otto's famous words, we stand in awe of the *mysterium tremendum*, the great mystery.[3] And there is an ethical dimension. We know that nature, just like human beings, should not be regarded as a means to an end.

In using the term "sacred," we recognize that there is something transcendent here, something that confers meaning and absolute worth to the thing or experience, something real that we humans are incapable of inventing. Generally, people have understood this intuition of transcendence as some form of divinity. ("Sacred," or *kadosh* in Hebrew, is applied to many things and activities; what it actually means is "connected to God.")

Yes, my secular reader might be thinking, but what does that have to do with the God of the Hebrew Bible, who demands loyalty and worship like a megalomaniac king, who torments Job on a whim and condemns Saul for refusing to kill children? If God is in charge, how come bad things happen to good people? And what about all the wars and massacres driven by religious identification?

These are not easy questions. I do not have any easy answers. Certainly I have no need or desire to defend the horrifying crimes against humanity perpetrated in the name of religion. I can only offer a few thoughts as to the wisdom of pursuing one's spiritual quest in the context of Judaism.

LOOKING FOR GOD

While religion has often gone astray, what prompts religion is real and enduring. It is the awe we feel in nature, the connection in a moment of love, the outrage in the face of injustice. It is transcendence. And unless we choose to live in an unpopulated part of Patagonia, the religious impulse will find social expression. The question isn't about whether organized religion should exist. It will always exist in one form or another. The real question is how to get it right.

Further, if I take my experience of transcendence seriously and want to make it a central part of my life, I need access to spiritual wisdom and fellow travelers on the path. Even if I could reinvent the spirituality wheel, it would likely be impoverished if all I had were my own experience and ideas. It makes sense to consult the wisdom of a tradition that has been working on transcendence for thousands of years. And unless one plans on conducting their spiritual search in a library, one needs teachers and fellow practitioners. We need to be exposed to many practices and ideas to find our way.

I did not become a rabbi to defend this Hebrew practice or that Jewish belief. I became a rabbi to further my spiritual quest. Perhaps fundamentalists feel otherwise. But I think I speak for most Orthodox Jews and certainly most liberal Jews when I say that more than preserving tradition, we are driven by the search for truth: true beliefs about the world, true spiritual practices that connect us to transcendence and develop our virtues, true friendships that nurture our hearts, true community that seeks justice for itself and others.

I do not need to validate all of Judaism. This is good because it would be impossible anyway. A biblical priest, a medieval rationalist, and a Hasidic mystic would agree on little about God. But what they offer today's spiritual seeker is an enormous compendium of wisdom and practices through which to engage the great spiritual questions of our time.

Finally, although Jews are among the most educated people in Western countries, most of them end their study of Judaism with bar or bat mitzvah. Often they think Judaism has an infantile view of God because the last time they seriously discussed it with a Jewish teacher, they were children. In reality, the variety and richness of Jewish God-talk is incredible. It's stunning. The Kabbalah (the dominant school of Jewish mysticism), for instance, is so outrageous and daring that if you did not know better, you would assume that anybody loyal to the Torah would consider it heretical. It is very likely that you will find something of your own experience of divinity in the teachings of the rabbis.

So I invite you to come explore with me in the next chapter, as I share some of my own spiritual search in the context of Judaism.

FINDING GOD
IN NATURE

Holy, holy, holy!
Adonai of the multitudes, whose glory fills the entire world.[1]

Isaiah 6:3

[To the ancient Israelites] God is not outside nature so much
as unfathomably deep within it: the essence of nature.

Evan Eisenberg[2]

For our biblical ancestors, the place of nature in spiritual practice was central. But today's Judaism is quite different from Temple-centered, ancient Israelite religion. Are there postbiblical rabbis and Jewish thinkers who agree with the biblical perspective on God and the natural world? If so, how did they interpret and update the worldview of the ancient Israelites? Can Jewish tradition provide us with a vocabulary to articulate our experience of wild nature as sacred and divine?

WONDER AND AWE:
ABRAHAM JOSHUA HESCHEL

Perhaps the most revered twentieth-century Jewish thinker in America is Abraham Joshua Heschel (1907–1972). Many

American institutions bear his name, particularly Jewish day schools. Born in Poland, Heschel received a classical Jewish education before studying for his doctorate in Germany. He came to America in 1939, rescued by Reform Judaism's rabbinical seminary, the Hebrew Union College. He quickly moved to New York, where he taught at the Conservative Movement's Jewish Theological Seminary. His popular book *The Sabbath* and his theological works made him famous in religious circles in the 1950s. In the 1960s Heschel burst onto the national scene as one of the first major religious figures in America to oppose the Vietnam War and support the civil rights movement. In the footage of Martin Luther King marching into Selma, the man at his shoulder with the goatee and flowing white hair is Heschel.

Heschel's magnum opus on Jewish theology is entitled *God in Search of Man*. (Heschel wrote in the 1950s; he surely would have embraced nonsexist language had he written later.) It covers the themes that any serious work on Jewish theology must: the revelation at Sinai, the authority of Jewish law, the problem of evil. But he only reaches those subjects on page 167! Part 1 is dedicated to the universal, human experience that religion is built upon. In particular, he devotes chapters to "wonder" and "awe" and gives us a new theological category: radical amazement.

THE WILL TO WONDER

I emerge from the tunnel on the road from Wawona and suddenly Yosemite Valley stands before me in all its glory. El Capitan towers to the left, Bridalveil Fall plunges to my right, Half Dome looks over it all from the center. I have seen it many times, but here I am again, astounded and ecstatic. What Heschel calls the *grandeur* of nature envelops me. I am filled with wonder.

Heschel teaches that wonder is different from curiosity. At this moment I am not interested in the geology of the valley. Maybe later. But now, enraptured by the natural world, my wonder does not lead to a set of questions that might be answered through scientific inquiry. Knowing how certain visual stimuli cause synaptic responses in the brain neither explains my amazement nor satisfies the longing in my heart. I don't want to ask how or why; I just want to say thanks.

This wonderful, that is, wonder-filled mystery, says Heschel, is what brings one to God.

> Awareness of the divine begins with wonder. It is the result of what man does with his higher incomprehension. The greatest hindrance to such awareness is our adjustment to conventional notions, to mental clichés. Wonder or radical amazement, the state of maladjustment to words and notions, is therefore a prerequisite for an authentic awareness of that which is.[3]

Wonder is that way of being in the world when we can truly be surprised, when, like children, we are not imprisoned by our past notions of the way things are supposed to be. Heschel, whose prose reads like poetry, would be the last one to disparage the value of words. But when it comes to the awareness of God, satisfaction with words and dogmas are more likely to blind than enlighten.

> As civilization advances, the sense of wonder declines. Such decline is an alarming symptom of our state of mind. Mankind will not perish for want of information; but only for want of appreciation. The beginning of our happiness lies in the understanding that life without wonder is not worth living. What we lack is not a will to believe but a will to wonder.[4]

This last line is Heschel's quintessentially Jewish response to the "leap of faith" theology prevalent in parts of the Christian world. William James famously wrote that one requires "the will to believe" because by contemporary intellectual standards, belief is a calculated risk.[5] Heschel counters, we need the "will to wonder." To find God, we don't need to avert our eyes from the world we know and what science teaches about it. Rather we need to look at it deeply—with "eyes remade for wonder."[6] Normally, one thinks of wonder as a reaction to something we see in the world around us. But Heschel claims that it is much more than that.

> To the prophets wonder is *a form of thinking* … it is an attitude that never ceases.[7]

This point is critical. Wonder happens to us. It is a gift we receive in the presence of beauty and grandeur. But the religious personality does not wait passively for it to happen again. Rather, she internalizes it as a value. She works to cultivate wonder as a virtue. This is the goal of a spiritual practice. The attitude of radical amazement enables her to experience more and more wonder in the world.

AWE: THE ROOT OF FAITH

Wonder or radical amazement, in turn, leads to awe. In our time, "awesome" is a word used far too glibly. It points to nothing less than the most precious moments in our lives. Awe is a response to beauty and grandeur, a recognition of mystery, an expression of humility.

Originally, the Hebrew word *yirah* meant "fear." But over time it came to denote "awe" as well. The two meanings are connected. The paradigmatically awesome moments of life, such as childbirth, are filled with danger. The mystery, fragility, and preciousness of our existence pervades awe-filled moments. The difference is that when we feel fear, say from a lightning storm, we want to run. When we feel awe, we want to stick around. We are attracted. Despite the danger, we even want to get closer.[8]

What does this mean to our spiritual sensitivities? No one can explain it better than Heschel.

The meaning of awe is to realize that life takes place under wide horizons, horizons that range beyond the span of an individual life or even the life of a nation, a generation, or an era. Awe enables us to perceive in the world intimations of the divine, to sense in small things the beginning of infinite significance, to sense the ultimate in the common and the simple; to feel in the rush of the passing the stillness of the eternal.[9]

For Heschel, wonder flows into awe, where we will ultimately meet the divine. In awe we know that the most physical things—rivers, flowers, mountains—point to the transcendent.

The experience of awe, so readily available in the natural world, is critical to Heschel's theology.

Awe precedes faith; it is *at the root of faith*. We must grow in awe in order to reach faith. We must be guided by awe to be worthy of faith. Awe rather than faith is the cardinal attitude of the religious Jew.[10]

It's so difficult to talk about the who and what of God. Often the same words mean different things to different people, and our conversations get bogged down in contradictions and misunderstanding. But when I say that I have "God-moments" in wilderness, people know exactly what I mean. In his description of radical amazement, Heschel captures this experience. When we are awestruck, the question of God is not contrived. If you ask, "Is this sacred?" you have already missed the point. We don't need to be "believers" in this or that dogma. Rather, we need to be people who see the world with "eyes of wonder."

Before Heschel, I always thought of wonder and awe as human reactions, something we cannot control. It did not occur to me that some people experience it more than others or that we can consciously try to make awe and wonder happen rather than wait for them to happen to us. But, of course, this is true. If awe is an attitude, then we can educate and train ourselves to acquire it. It is the aim of spiritual practice. We'll be returning to the dynamics of this process throughout *A Wild Faith*.

WILDERNESS: THE GATEWAY TO EVERYDAY AWE

Heschel was famous for beginning a lecture by exclaiming, "I have just seen a miracle! I have just seen a miracle! I have seen the sunset." It is not surprising, for Heschel teaches that the path to God is through awe, and nature is the most reliable gateway.

In explicating the dynamics of awe—beauty, grandeur, fear, danger, attraction, humility, mystery—Heschel explains why wilderness is indeed awesome. In the backcountry, beauty is commanding and pervasive. But so is danger and risk. One cannot see wildflowers or moose calves without passing rotting tree trunks, the remains of fire, or unburied bones. The grandeur and fragility of our world, the immediacy of life and death, are all around. It's hard *not* to feel awe in wilderness.

And awe opens our eyes and hearts to God's presence. In awesome moments, the great mystery of our lives holds us like a baby.

THE RIVER OF LIGHT: JEWISH MYSTICISM

A second source of spiritual wisdom that illuminates the experience of wild nature as sacred is Jewish mystical thought. Appearances to the contrary, mysticism isn't much of a mystery. While mystical thought admirably recognizes limits to human knowledge in its very name, it is a misleading term for a theology. Mysticism is simply one of many religious takes on how the world works. It claims some things and refutes others. But it says just as much, probably more, about the big issues of God, revelation, and human nature as any other stream of spiritual thinking.

"HORIZONTAL" THEOLOGY

In the Western religions, the major difference between mainstream and mystical theology is what scholars have called a "horizontal," as opposed to a "vertical," approach to God. Traditionally, God is conceived as a superbeing living far off in heaven. Generally hidden, God breaks through to the human level in rare but dramatic fashion (as in the descent to Mount Sinai in fire and smoke) to exceptional human beings (the prophets), though each of us can connect to God on some level through prayer.

How different for the mystics! To them, God is perceived as part of Being itself—in all things at all times. To quote an analogy oft used by mystics, imagine that God is an ocean and people are like waves. Waves are individual and distinct from other parts of the ocean and other waves, but never separate, for they cannot exist apart from the ocean. And when the winds die down, the individual waves recede and merge with the sea. This is the mystics' spiritual goal: to become entirely one with God.

Mysticism reinterprets traditional Western religion in radical ways. Instead of beseeching God above (hence, "vertical" theology), we turn to God ("horizontally") by looking within and looking around. Rather than residing in a remote or hidden abode, God is always here, in ourselves and in the world around us. This leads to a startling reversal of traditional theology. Revelation is less dependent on God than people. If God is not present to us, it is because we fail to see what is right before our eyes.

What blinds us to God? Our individual existence, if not an illusion, is an impediment to our spiritual development, for at our very core we are part of God. The mystic's aim is to shed one's "false" self, our self-centered egos, in order to merge and rest in our true nature, that is, in God. The onus, then, is on the person to overcome one's egoism, for God is always waiting for us in the world and in our hearts.

Hasidic rabbis, who adopted and adapted Jewish mysticism from the mid-eighteenth century onwards, speak of *mochin d'katnut*, small-mindedness or small consciousness, and its opposite, *mochin d'gadlut*.[11] In expanded consciousness, we fulfill God's will because the godly part of us is directing our thoughts and actions.

Taken to its extreme, this leads to even more revolutionary insights. When one teaches Torah in *mochin d'gadlut*, when all self-awareness has dissolved, the godly part of a person emerges. The teacher is an empty vessel filled with God's spirit. Then it is not the teacher who is teaching Torah, but God! This is even more outrageous with regard to prayer. When one prays in expanded consciousness, God, as it were, is praying to God![12]

For the mystic, a key element of spiritual life is the ability to become an empty vessel that God can fill.

JEWISH MYSTICISM: THE KABBALAH

The Jewish mystical tradition known as the Kabbalah grew exponentially during the late Middle Ages, primarily in Islamic lands. The most famous of the many kabbalistic books, the *Zohar*, was written in thirteenth-century Spain. This is not coincidental. While Europe languished through the Dark Ages, human knowledge continued to advance in Arab culture.

As would later happen in Christian Europe during the Renaissance, Islamic thought was driven by the discovery of ancient Greek thought. Jewish philosophy began in earnest as rabbis in Muslim lands responded to the thinking of their Islamic counterparts. They understood God in a new way—on the basis of logical argument—as perfect, unchanging, and wholly spiritual. The familiar notions to us of God as all-knowing, all-powerful, and all-good date back to this time. While great rabbis such as Maimonides (the "second Moses," twelfth century, Egypt) embraced the new science with open arms, others were less enthusiastic. How could the unmoved mover, the God of the philosophers, notice individual people and answer prayers? How did purely spiritual God enter this material world at all? Kabbalah took up the challenge.

Instead of saying "yes/no," the kabbalists responded "yes/and." God, they taught, is indeed beyond all human comprehension and experience, transcendent and removed from our world. Their primary name for God is *Ein Sof:* the One without end, unlimited and ultimately unknowable. In fact, they surpass the philosophers in their recognition of the utterly transcendent nature of God. But at the same time, they never questioned the immanent, personal God of the Hebrew Bible. How they held on to both poles is the genius of Kabbalah.

THE *SHEFA*, THE DIVINE FLOW

The kabbalists presented an entirely new understanding of the creation of the world, a prequel to the Book of Genesis. Their thinking reached its definitive form in the thought of Rabbi Isaac Luria (sixteenth century, Palestine). The Lurianic story of creation goes like this.

In the beginning, all was God, all was *Ein Sof,* the One without limits. In order to create the universe, God first needed to withdraw part of God's self to make room for something else. Then, the *Ein Sof* emanated divine light from Itself into the vacated space. The light acquired more and more solidity as it traveled through the void, forming the universe. Of the many innovations introduced by kabbalists, this one is profound for present-day environmentalists. The whole universe is made of God-stuff.

The famous kabbalistic chart of the ten spheres, the ten aspects of God, represents this creation process. As God's light "descended," God's being became more and more tangible. God's spiritual aspects came into the universe: understanding and wisdom, then love, mercy, and judgment. Finally, as God's light became denser, the lowest, tenth sphere was created, which includes the physical world we inhabit. Some kabbalists referred to this last sphere as *Shechinah*, an earlier rabbinic term to denote God's presence in the world. Derived from the Hebrew root *sh-ch-n* (dwelling), *Shechinah* names God's immanence in the world. For the kabbalists, *Shechinah* is a feminine aspect of divinity.

This perception of God is indeed hard to comprehend. Scholars use the awkward term "godhead" to convey the idea that God is made up of many different spheres or aspects. But this is why Kabbalah can hold on to the poles of God as impersonal, transcendent spirit, the *Ein Sof*, and God as *Shechinah*, the immanent, personal God who animates the material world and affects human beings. When God acts in the world, judging human actions or answering prayers, it is the "lower," more tangible aspects of divinity that interact with people.

But the most daring part of Kabbalah concerns the converse. What humans do affects God.

While the details vary among kabbalists, they agree on this basic point: God's emanation is likened to a river, a River of Light, that continually flows into the universe. Were it to stop, the universe would cease to exist. This divine flow, or *shefa* in Hebrew, is a two-way street. What humans do sends divine energy back "up" the ladder of the ten spheres, provoking a reaction from the appropriate, divine sphere. Committing evil draws out judgment from the godhead, increasing the amount of strict justice flowing in the stream, whereas following the commandments and practicing good increases mercy and loving-kindness. People affect the composition of the divine flow, which in turn affects people. We humans "actualize" the River of Light.

God's ability to influence the world, then, is radically dependent on human action. Spirit not only moves us, we move spirit! We can change God! This is the origin of the modern meaning of *tikkun olam* as "repairing the world."

BECOMING A MYSTIC

Now all this talk of God as River of Light and "godhead" sounds fantastical and bizarre, especially if you have not heard it before. True, Lurianic Kabbalah is the only premodern cosmology that foresaw a scenario similar to the big bang.[13] But what does the Lurianic creation story have to do with us? Why turn to such out- rageous medieval speculation for truth when we have the reason- able and increasingly proven accounts of modern science? I dismissed Kabbalah as nonsense for most of my adult life.

Things began to change for me around the time of my ordi- nation, just as I was rediscovering wilderness. As a student in Jerusalem, I needed exercise. In addition to my weekly floor hockey game, I turned to two spiritual body practices: Yoga and Tai Chi. Both felt great. I was also impressed by friends who ben- efited from acupuncture treatments and enjoyed some myself.

So I respected and benefited from these Eastern body prac- tices. Deep into Western philosophy as I wrote my rabbinic thesis, however, I had no interest in the ideas behind them. I chose teach- ers who didn't bother me with talk of chakras or energy meridians in the body. "Energy" was a buzzword that seemed to apply to everything (and therefore nothing) to the New Agers I politely dismissed.

But it quickly occurred to me that the most plausible expla- nation for what I was experiencing in the desert had to do with energy. My body had a buzz or a charge to it in wilderness. I remembered the energy theory behind Chinese medicine, how I respected acupuncture, and how relaxed yet alive and alert I felt during Tai Chi.

And then I was reminded of Kabbalah's basic premise when I read Rabbi Lawrence Kushner's book *The River of Light* (Jewish Lights). God enters the world as a *shefa*, a continual flow of divine light or energy streaming into the universe. I noticed that the Hasidic term for this life-force, *chiut* (from the same root as *chaim*, "life"), sounds like the Chinese word for energy: *chi*. No doubt a coincidence, but it got me to ask: Was I feeling *chiut* in the desert?

After taking the Israeli desert guide's course, I began to explore spirituality in wilderness more seriously. I craved any book that could shed light on what I was experiencing. I searched for teachers of spirituality, particularly in nature, a search that eventually led me back to the United States after fifteen years in Israel.

At that time, in 1998, Buddhist meditation teacher (and faithful Jew) Sylvia Boorstein began to bring the fruits of her mindfulness[14] practice to rabbis in America. After a four-day meditation retreat, I asked her how to pursue the practice more seriously. A few months later, I began a six-week silent retreat at her Buddhist home, the Spirit Rock Meditation Center, and followed it with a four-week sit a year later.

Vipassana or Insight meditation is nonprogrammatic meditation. One does not visualize letters or images, concentrate on a candle flame, or repeat a mantra. Rather, it is pure mindfulness. In sitting meditation, you close your eyes and then pay close attention to the most prominent sensation (usually the breath) and later your various mental states.

My body awareness increased a hundredfold. I closely observed my body's interaction with emotions, desires, and different kinds of thoughts. I saw how the body responds to audio and tactile stimuli. And I learned a very valuable truth. While the mind has many ruses, the body does not lie. If my mind was thinking happy thoughts and my body was tense, I was likely in denial about something. I learned how much of what we think of as intuition is really a bodily reaction to the situation, a lesson that made sense of what I felt when hiking in the desert. I learned to trust what I was feeling on my skin.

At the same time, I began a series of solo wilderness retreats, loosely patterned on the Native American "vision quest," with a teacher named John Milton. The practice involves spending four days in wilderness alone in a small circle, fasting from food and engaging in various forms of prayer and meditation.

While John brings his Native American heritage to the table, he teaches out of deep experience in both Daoism and Tibetan Buddhism. He is a master of Tai Chi and an experienced meditator. I wanted to see how he brought those practices to spiritual expression in wilderness. I wasn't disappointed.

After four days of preparation with John in a group, I settled into my "Soul-O" site near a creek in the Sangre de Cristo mountains in Colorado. (For an explanation of "Soul-O" sites, see practice 9.) No forms of entertainment were allowed—no reading, no journaling, no photographing. We were after heightened, sustained awareness of the natural world, as pure a state of mindfulness as possible. I meditated on stones and water and stars and the space between the stars. My usual impatience gave way to stillness. One night I faced the moon for hours in standing meditation while it traveled from one side of a pine tree to the other.

But for me, John's most important teachings concerned the energies in nature. What Chinese medicine teaches about the energy meridians in the body is also true of the earth as a whole. Just as different materials serve as better or worse conductors of electricity, *chi* is channeled through the earth by the different elements. In addition, each thing in nature, particularly living things, carries a distinct vibration or energy that with proper sensitivity can be sensed by humans.

John taught us Chi Quong, Daoist body meditation, to develop that sensitivity and strengthen our own *chi*. I learned to absorb *chi* by meditating in spots where the energy was strongest and learned how to exchange *chi* with trees. My skepticism melted away as I was literally energized. I was feeling the "buzz" I normally felt in nature, only now ten times stronger.

If you had told me that three years after finishing my rabbinic thesis on the intersection of Western philosophy and liberal Jewish theology, I'd be "talking" to a tree, I would have had quite a laugh. But there was no denying my experience.

BECOMING A JEWISH MYSTIC

The Chinese see *chi* as a force, more or less like electricity or gravity. Steeped in the God-expectations of Judaism and the God-language of Kabbalah, I thought it might be more than that. I began to experiment with Jewish prayer and what I had learned about myself and the natural world through mindfulness and Chi Quong. I embraced the energies of the natural world not only as *chi*, but as *chiut*.

I was inspired by the teachings and prayers of the Hasidic master and mystic Rabbi Nachman of Breslov (1772–1811), who uses the term *chiut* frequently. Hasidic theology in general, and his in particular, boldly interpreted Kabbalah for European Jews in early modern times.

> Know that every shepherd has a unique *nigun* [melody] according to the grasses and the place where he herds.... For every grass there is a song which it speaks, and from the song of the grasses is made the *nigun* of the shepherd.[15]

> Master of the Universe, grant me the ability to be alone; may it be my custom to go outdoors each day among the trees and grass—among all growing things—and there may I be alone, and enter into prayer, to talk with the One to whom I belong. May I express there everything in my heart, and may all the foliage of the field—all grasses, trees and plants—awake at my coming, to send the powers of their life into the words of my prayer so that my prayer and speech are made whole through the life and spirit of all growing things....[16]

Three years earlier, I considered this pure rubbish. Now, I felt that I was experiencing exactly what moved Rabbi Nachman! I wasn't just enjoying the view in wilderness. I was feeling the divine life-force. My prayer and meditation gathered the *chiut*, sent it streaming through my veins, and channeled it back into creation.

If all I knew was mainstream Jewish theology, I would have had real qualms about pursuing these practices as a Jew. But the very Kabbalah that had seemed so out of touch with reality not only assuaged my Jewish authenticity fears, it offered the most plausible explanation of what I was experiencing.

The metaphor of God as a River of Light that animates the earth jibes with my experience of divinity in the world. In this image, the *shefa* (divine flow) is likened to a river and *chiut* (divine life-force) is likened to water in the river. *Chiut* is strongest in the natural world, where life is abundant and even rocks channel the *shefa* in a way concrete and plastic do not. It explains why I generally feel closer to God in nature than in buildings; why I feel energized in a forest and depressed in a parking lot. It makes sense both of Chi Quong and Rabbi Nachman. And what the never-ending flow or *shefa* of divine light infuses, the earth we inhabit, is itself made of god-stuff. No wonder I experience the natural world as sacred and holy.

It is shocking to think of God as a force rather than a person,[17] but especially for those who have trouble with traditional images of God, it opens up intriguing possibilities. If God relates to the world more as a push than a pull—a dynamic, catalyzing energy in the world—then evolution makes sense. Nothing is preordained, the world is open-ended and constantly in flux, human choice is truly free. Yet this force is intelligent, demanding our ethical responsibility, and showering us with never-ending love and compassion. What we call "evil" is either the necessary processes of the natural world (earthquakes, hurricanes) or human choices made not because of God's presence in the world, but despite it. Whether or not we receive God's love depends on our ability to open our hearts and become a vessel for God's spirit.

"*I* AND *THOU* ": MARTIN BUBER

Martin Buber's (1878–1965) voice still reverberates decades after his death. He was born to an assimilated family in Vienna, but due to his parents' separation, he was raised in rural Galicia by his extraordinary grandfather. Solomon Buber was not only a farmer, he published critical editions of ancient Hebrew manuscripts! Young Martin was exposed to nature as well as to both modern scholarship and traditional Jewish culture. With his grandfather, he even made occasional visits to a Hasidic rebbe.

Buber rose to prominence in widely different fields before World War I. A contemporary of Theodor Herzl, he was an important leader in the early Zionist movement. As a writer and social commentator, he edited a countercultural journal that published a who's who of German intellectual thought. Like many of his generation, Buber's spiritual quest led to mysticism. He edited collections of mystical writings from around the world and gained general fame by translating Hasidic texts into German, putting Hasidism on the European cultural map.

But Buber is most famous for his little book, *I and Thou.* Published shortly after World War I, Buber's ideas about dialogue altered the cultural landscape of Europe, influencing Christians even more than Jews.

I and Thou is a conscious rejection of mysticism. In fact, he came to the idea of I-Thou by critiquing his own mystical beliefs (though he retains much from mystical thought in his "dialogical theology"). In his memoir, "Autobiographical Fragments,"[18] Buber recounts an incident that illustrates his change of heart. Just before World War I, Buber was engaged in his mystical practice when a student came to speak with him. Buber relates that he listened politely but without sufficient attention to discern why the troubled student had approached him. The next he heard, the student had died at the front. Remorseful, Buber thought deeply about a spirituality that prodded the practitioner to retreat from the world.[19]

The result was *I and Thou*, published in 1923. It is a philosophy and theology of engagement with the world. The main premise is deceptively simple. People are always relating to the world in one of two basic ways: I-Thou or I-It.

A case of I-It: I approach a teller at a bank. We exchange pleasantries while my transactions are conducted, and then I leave. I have just spoken with a human being, but I might as well have been speaking to an ATM.

A case of I-Thou: A parent listening intently to discern the needs of a newborn infant. Or touching your partner and knowing that you are in love. Or listening deeply to another's words, talking through differences, and coming to a truer understanding. Or looking into another's eyes and feeling their pain as your own.

In I-It mode, my exchanges with the world serve some purpose. I analyze a problem to come up with a solution; I speak to the teller to conduct a transaction; I follow the traffic lights to avoid an accident. This is the world of subjects and objects, of means and ends.

In a moment of I-Thou, rather than imposing my agenda, I am listening to the other. I have no expectations as to what is supposed to happen; I have no idea where this encounter will take me; preconceptions and prejudices have been left behind. Yet I know that this is critical. This is where the real and true me will emerge. This is the world of relation.

Buber knew that for the most part, we must live in I-It. He claimed, however, that the quality of our lives is determined by how we respond to moments of I-Thou. If Buber is correct, then the better we understand I-Thou, the better we understand the most significant times of our lives. For me, the following aspects are particularly salient.

Only You, All of You—In Buber's words, when we are in I-Thou, the Thou "fills the horizon." The rest of the world has not disappeared, but we no longer see it. Our attention is total. We are engrossed and enraptured by the Thou. Quite literally, I am all ears. And what we see is the other in that person's completeness. When I approach a person in I-It consciousness, I might ask: Could this person help me get a job? Could he help me with my chemistry assignment? Or even, how does the central nervous system work? In I-Thou, I do not ask what the other is useful for or break him or her down into parts for the purpose of analysis. I take the person in as a whole, just as he or she is.

The Eternal Now—When we enter I-Thou relationship, a window of transcendence—what Buber calls the "Eternal Now"—opens in the very midst of the time-space universe we occupy. I-Thou breaks down subject/object dualism and creates a new unity, the relation between the I and the Thou. Buber calls this newly opened realm where relation occurs the "Between."

The Eternal One—It is in the Between that God becomes real and presses "over and against" us. We encounter the Eternal One in the Eternal Now. This is perhaps the most difficult part of Buber's thought to comprehend. Buber refused to talk about what God is, only what it is like to meet the divine. We are so used to thinking of God as a discrete being, whether corporeal or incorporeal, that we have trouble thinking of God as overlapping with and permeating human beings and their actions. But for Buber, like the kabbalists and the River of Light, God touches us when we are touched by the world around us, that is, when we enter into genuine or I-Thou relationship. In Buber's words, "The extended lines of relations meet in the Eternal Thou."[20]

Communion, Love, and the Commanding Thou—Why do some people experience I-Thou frequently, while others hardly at all? I-Thou relation demands our response-ability. To enter I-Thou, I first confirm the other as a Thou, as one I cannot use as a means to an end. If I cannot respect the other, that person cannot become a Thou to my I. Usually, I-Thou is an expression of spontaneous love and empathy. I feel the needs of my Thou as my own. Honoring and protecting my Thou goes without saying; justice and compassion are not optional. English captures well what Buber has in mind. Response-ability becomes responsibility for the Thou. I-Thou is the source and catalyst of the ethical life.

The Authentic Life—It is in moments of I-Thou that we feel most alive. We know love; we hear the demand to live ethically. They lead to self-discovery and authentic living. In other words, these are our most significant and meaningful moments. The more we have, the better our lives.

While the paradigmatic I-Thou encounter is between two people, Buber writes that we also encounter spiritual realities, such as ideas or artistic inspiration. We can encounter a text like the Torah in I-Thou fashion. And most important for us, I-Thou relations are also possible between people and other living beings. In "Autobiographical Fragments," Buber shares that one of the first I-Thou encounters he remembers was between himself and a horse on his grandfather's farm.[21] At the very beginning of *I and Thou*, Buber offers a description of an I-Thou encounter with a tree.

In it, Buber summarizes the many ways one can view a tree: as a series of motions and movements, as an object of biological study, as an expression of physical laws, as a tree in a larger forest.

In all this the tree remains my object, occupies space and time, and has its nature and constitution.

It can, however, also come about, if I have both will and grace, that in considering the tree I become bound up in relation to it. The tree is no longer *It*. I have been seized by the power of exclusiveness.

To effect this it is not necessary for me to give up any of the ways in which I consider the tree. There is nothing from which I would have to turn my eyes away in order to see, and no knowledge that I would have to forget. Rather is everything, picture and movement, species and type, law and number, indivisibly united in this event.

Everything belonging to the tree is in this: its form and structure, its colours and chemical composition, its intercourse with the elements and with the stars, are all present in a single whole.

The tree is no impression, no play of my imagination, no value depending on my mood; but it is bodied over against me and has to do with me, as I with it—only in a different way.

Let no attempt be made to sap the strength from the meaning of the relation: relation is mutual.

The tree will have a consciousness, then, similar to our own? Of that I have no experience.... I encounter no soul or dryad [a "tree spirit"] of the tree, but the tree itself.[22]

Notice that nearly all the elements of I-Thou relation between people are also present here. As you might imagine, Buber was widely criticized for extending dialogue to animals and trees. But he remained faithful to the truth of his experience.

RECEPTIVE MODE
One of my favorite Buber commentators is Harvard professor of education Nel Noddings. Her book *Caring: A Feminine Approach to Ethics and Moral Education*[23] is a sustained meditation on

(paradoxically) the man, Buber, who provides the basic suppositions of her thinking. Noddings seeks to explain the role of I-Thou in the regular, commonplace events of our lives. She offers the following interpretation.

Imagine yourself before a giant jigsaw puzzle. You open your eyes wide, empty your mind, and wait for an idea. Noddings calls this mental state "receptive mode." Then inspiration hits. You have an idea; you see a pattern. You start moving pieces and try it out. This is "analytic mode." We organize the world in our minds and impose our will to arrange it according to our needs. If the solution works, great. If it doesn't, we spread the pieces out again and start over. It is more difficult now, as we have to forget the idea that did not work. Emptying the mind is not easy. We relax, take a breath, and enter as deeply as possible into receptive mode in order to take in the widest possible view and receive another idea.

Receptive mode is the mental state we enter before and during moments of I-Thou. We take in the other as a whole, free ourselves as much as possible from the preconceptions and prejudices of our past, and listen as deeply as possible. In "analytic mode," in I-It consciousness, we break things into parts and manipulate the world according to our purposes.

In his philosophic writings, Buber tends to describe I-Thou in dramatic terms. Like Moses at the burning bush, the Thou takes him by surprise.[24] The consequences of the encounter are far-reaching. But in his writings on Hasidism, Buber emphasizes the everyday side of I-Thou relation.[25] And this is particularly important to the experience of I-Thou in the natural world. I am not amazed at the beauty of a lupine flower every time I pass one. Seeing a squirrel for the 2,475th time does not rock my world. In fact, I often pass by them in I-It consciousness. It is a struggle not to take things for granted. But with proper attention, with "eyes remade for wonder," I can enter receptive mode and experience I-Thou at any time.

Noddings captures this part of Buber's message. She shows us that I-Thou need not be a paradigm-shifting, life-changing event. Next to "big" I-Thou events, "little" I-Thou moments occur on a regular basis. Each of us enters receptive mode frequently in a given day. Receptive mode is akin to *mochin d'gadlut*, the state of expanded consciousness that Hasidic rabbis praise, the state of seeing the sacred in every person, thing, and action. In *mochin d'gadlut*, we see everything in the world as a potential Thou.

Receptive mode is a term I will return to frequently. It is almost identical to mindfulness. At its core, it is pure and simple listening. Since receptive mode literally keeps us open to new experience, it gives us the best chance of responding to the potential Thous that might come our way. Finally, mindfulness is something that can be taught. For me, it is a central goal of Jewish spiritual practice in wilderness.

ETERNITY IS HERE AND NOW

I have found very few people who disagree with Buber's basic premise regarding I-Thou versus I-It, myself included. These are the moments that make life worth living. Much of Heschel's description of awe coheres with Buber's insights into I-Thou relation.

In moments of I-Thou, eternity—the transcendence of time, space, and self—opens to us in the midst of time, space, and self. For me, this is the most fascinating and critical part of Buber's thought for Jews who perceive wilderness as sacred and holy. It makes sense of what I regularly experience in wilderness but what Western thought, with its strict separation of body and mind and spirit and matter, says should not happen. I find spirit and transcendence with eyes open in the most material and physical of places.

In *I and Thou*, Buber imparts a powerful explanation as to how people experience divinity in nature—not around it, through it, or despite it, but *in* it. God is easy to miss. Most people do. But when we genuinely encounter wilderness, the sacred and transcendent qualities of the natural world enrapture us. We feel God's love. We are ethically commanded. We are transformed.

INTO THE WILDERNESS

Jewish tradition and thought, we can conclude, indeed provides a rich conceptual vocabulary to articulate a Wilderness Jew's perception of the natural world as sacred. The rest of *A Wild Faith* is devoted to integrating the insights of the above teachers into Jewish spiritual practice in wilderness.

It would not be correct, however, to think that each of our teachers would endorse every practice in this book. They differed widely in their perceptions of divinity and observance. Heschel's conception of God is quite traditional; the mystics and Buber locate God's actual presence in this world. Heschel and the mystics were traditionally observant; Buber was not. But together with the Hebrew Bible, our teachers have raised a tent in which Wilderness Jews from across the theological spectrum can take shelter.

Those of us who find our most profound God-moments in the natural world often feel like we're swimming upstream in the Jewish world. While this may be the current reality in Jewish institutional life, we are not, in fact, challenging the foundational tenets of Judaism. The opposite is true. We are returning to our biblical roots through contemporary God-talk. We are digging down to the bedrock of Jewish belief and claiming our inheritance.

A MAP OF
THE HEART

It would usually take several days on the trail to leave behind the weight of my ego, my self-consciousness and all that is familiar and routine, and free my mind. In these moments, the world opened up to me; I felt an intimacy with the earth, I was more aware of the plants' special habits, I laughed easily and was eager to chat with strangers. I felt a profound generosity toward the world that comes too infrequently in my daily life.

Ellen Bernstein[1]

Jewish spiritual practice in wilderness is not an island. Before we jump into specific practices, it is important to locate wilderness spirituality in the wider context of spiritual practice in general and Judaism in particular. Doing so will lend perspective and coherence to the individual spiritual exercises in *A Wild Faith*, as each exercise contributes to the larger purposes of the overall practice. In spiritual practice, the whole is greater than its parts.

THE PURPOSE OF SPIRITUAL PRACTICE

Spiritual practice rarely comes easily. For most of us, it's a bumpy road with plenty of ups and downs, highs and lows, two steps forward and one step back. "Spiritual practice" is often used inter-changeably with "spiritual discipline," and for good reason. To make one's spiritual practice effective, and to accrue the benefits, takes dedication, effort, awareness, and continuity.

What are the benefits? It rarely takes me more than five minutes in the company of a spiritual teacher or practitioner to know if their practice is working. If it is, they are relaxed, hard to make angry, concerned about you and the world yet light-hearted and joyous, wise in a commonsense way, less caught up in material or cultural distractions, selfless, content, patient ... you get the idea. I'm sure you could add a few of your own. The point is that spiritual practice is not about accumulating a maximal number of minutes on the meditation cushion or completing a certain number of rituals. Practices are a means to an end, and that end is a kind of personality, a quality of the heart.

One of the paradoxes of spiritual life is that it rarely succeeds unless we give up the "inner critic," the need to make judgments about all that passes before us. And yet, we need to know that the difficulties of spiritual practice are worth overcoming. We need to know whether our own practice is succeeding.

If we are seeking a quality of the heart, however, the best measure is not whether we had this or that experience of transcendence, how much we sacrificed to help a friend, or how many letters we sent to Congress last month. These are important, but not always consistent yardsticks of spiritual practice. Rather, we can look at ourselves and ask, is my practice making me more aware, more responsible, more joyous, and more content? Am I becoming the kind of person whose practice makes a difference in his or her life? This involves emotions and attitudes as well as actions. We all know charitable people who treat their spouses poorly or whose emotional lives are a mess. Spiritual practice, including spiritual practice in wilderness, is meant to affect the whole person.

While we need to make these judgments, it is important to do so gently, with great compassion for the person we are often least likely to give it to—ourselves. Many beginning spiritual practitioners carry unrealistic expectations. They expect too much too fast. This, unfortunately, can lead people to give up before they experience the benefits of a spiritual path. After all, spiritual practice is challenging. It requires us to go beyond the behaviors that our society normally rewards. It might ask us to extend our most basic beliefs about what is real and what is possible. We might have to try things that are extremely difficult, some of which seem downright silly. We have to deal with our neuroses and fears.

But when the going gets tough, we need not throw in the towel. Most beginners suffer from a lack of perspective rather than a lack of ability. Remember, these things take time, and indeed, "big" I-Thou moments are rare. I have not met a person who tried spiritual practice over time and later regretted the investment.

This is one of the many reasons that spiritual practice is best learned with a teacher. It's less about ability than expectations.

THE JEWISH CONTEXT

Just as spirituality in wilderness is never really divorced from spirituality elsewhere, an effective Jewish spirituality in wilderness will fit into the larger practice of Judaism and one's particular Jewish community. So I'd like to mention the overall context of the specific practices in *A Wild Faith:* the major characteristics of Judaism as a spiritual path.

Many interpretations have been suggested as to the essence or bottom line of Judaism. In a tradition as old and rich as Judaism, they can be quite different from each other. One of my favorites is Hillel's famous reply to the gentile who asked him to describe Judaism while standing on one foot:

> What is hateful to you, do not do to your neighbor: that is the whole Torah; the rest is commentary; go, study.[2]

Another favorite is from the prophet Micah (6:8):

> He has told you, O man, what is good,
> And what Adonai requires of you:
> Only to do justice
> And to love goodness,
> And to walk modestly with your God....

Western religion is always an answer to the question: What does God want from us, and how do we do it? If I had to give a Jewish answer in three words (less pressure than one foot), I would say *kedushah* (holiness), *tikkun* (transformation), and *b'rit* (covenant).

KEDUSHAH—HOLINESS

Literally, "holiness" and its synonyms (sacred, blessed, hallowed) refer to the place or the time or the action in which we connect to divinity. It is when and where transcendence is real. And so it is notoriously difficult to describe.

On the one hand, *kedushah* is quite definable. It refers to that which is separated from the mundane and is connected to God. Holiness is intertwined with ethics. The famous command, "You shall be holy, for I, Adonai your God, am holy" (Lev. 19:2), is followed by the most sublime ethical passage in Torah: leave the corners of your harvest for the poor, protect the weak, judge fairly, don't place a stumbling block before the blind, don't exploit your workers, don't bear a grudge, disavow revenge, and love your neighbor as yourself (Lev. 19:9–18).

But at its core, holiness is a great mystery. It refers to that intangible feeling we have in the face of eternity. We sense the power of the moment, usually filled with light and emotion, which empowers us. Yet we feel humble. Intuiting both the grandeur and fragility of life, recognizing grace, we are grateful. Holiness is associated with awe because the holy and the sacred evoke awe.

Kedushah is a term favored by liberal rabbis because it allows us to talk about the experience of the sacred with people who, for whatever reasons, are uncomfortable with the word "God." The fact that fundamentalists use "God," "holy," and other terms in ways that horrify nonfundamentalists leads many religious liberals[3] to give up the core vocabulary of Jewish tradition. But that is throwing the baby out with the bath water. Unless we are willing to give up on the sacred, we need to find ways of using these terms without embarrassment or self-consciousness.

Kedushah, then, is the context and the goal of Jewish ritual and practice: to feel the sacred, to respond to it, to increase it. We will continue this discussion in chapters 8 and 9.

TIKKUN—TRANSFORMATION

When I look at the ethical injunctions, wisdom literature, and stories of the Hebrew Bible and Jewish law, together with the ritual practices of Judaism, I come to one conclusion. Judaism is about transformation: our world, our people, our country, our local communities, ourselves. This last item, ourselves, is perhaps the most difficult, even though it is where we exercise the most control, and it is perhaps the most important, in that most of us need to change ourselves if we are to help change the world.

Tikkun literally means to "fix" or "repair." The work of repairing the world needs to be done on every level, from the individual to the global village.

Most national identities in the Western world—Polish, English, Russian—were formed by living on a common land while speaking a common language. The societal bond is primarily historical. The fact that one's country was once a monarchy and now Communist, once totalitarian and now a democracy, once pagan and now Christian, is irrelevant to one's primary identity as a Romanian or a Spaniard or an Italian.

But two nations in Western history were created by identifying a common mission based on mutually held values, an eye to the future rather than the past. If you are an American Jew, you hit the jackpot. You are a member of both. Your national identity as an American and your ethnic/national[4] identity as a Jew were formed by conscious agreement.

Since its inception, however, American nationality has been normalized. Today one's birth in the United States is more important to American identity than a personal belief in the Bill of Rights. And the same is true to some extent of Jews, particularly Israelis. The fact of birth is more important to many than an allegiance to the Torah.

But if the Constitution were junked, something distinctly "American" would continue in North America. The same cannot be said of the Jewish people. We would not survive outside of Israel without the continuing dialogue with our sacred text. While Yiddish idioms, Jewish comedians, and good deli reflect a cultural reality, they cannot drive a dynamic Jewish culture. There is a reason that Jewish Community Centers are few and the synagogue remains the primary Jewish institution in the Diaspora. It seems clear to me that without conscious allegiance to the Torah among the masses of Jews, even on a nominal level, we would be gone in a generation.

And if you know anything about the Torah, you know you are commanded. The charge to become holy, to be pure of heart and morally honest, is not optional. You must strive to be better. If you take your Jewish identity with any degree of sincerity, your life's work is transformation.

It starts with the individual. But more important is the community and the world, because the Jewish people has always understood its own existence as an extension of the covenant with God.

B'RIT—COVENANT

The sun is just above the horizon when I light the Sabbath candles and begin to sing the *Kabbalat Shabbat*, Friday night service. In a minyan of pine trees next to an alpine lake in the backcountry of the Sierra, I welcome the Sabbath bride. Alone, I am anything but lonely. As I sing the melodies and daven the prayers, my people are all around me. I don't see them, but I am with them and they are with me. Jews have said these very same prayers for hundreds of years. All around the world, as the sun sets, Jews are gathering in their communities. We share the same ritual, the same language, the same history. We are all members of the *b'rit*, the covenant, the age-old marriage between God and the Jewish people. It started with Abraham and now, millennia later, despite the trials of a difficult history, it has survived and been gifted to me.

In Judaism, personal salvation is not the ultimate goal. The focus is communal. It is not the individual but the Jewish people and, ultimately, the entire world that will benefit if Jews respond to the demands of Judaism and hasten the coming of the Messiah. Messianism is different for different Jews. As a Reform Jew, I am not waiting for a messenger from God in the form of a person. Rather, I understand that it is my responsibility to practice *tikkun* and help bring about the messianic age, when peace will replace war and humanity will live in harmony with the natural world.

But the common point to all streams of Judaism is that Jewish spirituality, first and foremost, is communal. Even when I am alone, I am in community. The traditional prayers of petition (for health, wisdom, forgiveness) are written in "we" language rather than "I" language. On Yom Kippur, the individual asks forgiveness for all the sins of the community. There are no Jewish monasteries. The great mystical rabbis, who meditated in the middle of the night, mediated during the day, as they were also judges and community leaders. They fulfilled the same worldly commandments as every other Jew.

From the viewpoint of Judaism, a spirituality that leads to self-awareness and personal growth but removes one from society is deeply flawed. I wish to emphasize this point for two reasons beyond the obvious one that we must be engaged with the world in order to leave it a better place than we found it.

Part of the attraction to wilderness for many of us is the fact that we leave civilization behind. We love to get away from other people. Generally this is healthy, but not always. For some, wilderness is like whiskey to an alcoholic. They attempt to suppress their problems by getting "high" on nature, from pushing adrenaline by running the rapids, to the joy of communing with wildlife. But a wholesome wilderness spirituality is not about running from our problems; it's about healing them.

Second, most of the exercises in *A Wild Faith* are meant for individual practice. Communal institutions are precisely what we do not find in wilderness. It would be easy, then, to understand spiritual practice in wilderness as an alternative to communal modes of Jewish observance. Indeed, I do believe that personal prayer and other individual practices deserve greater emphasis in Jewish life. Overall, however, the goal is an engaged spirituality. If one follows the practices in *A Wild Faith* and is not moved to live a sustainable lifestyle, if one's spiritual growth in wilderness does not lead to better relationships in the city and increased sensitivity to those in need around the world—if spiritual practice in wilderness does not increase one's participation in communal activities— we deceive ourselves. The practice is skewed. We are likely flattering our egos and otherwise circumventing the areas of our spiritual life that we most need to explore.

I have to say, I'm not worried. My experience is that the more one explores Judaism in wilderness, the more meaningful and important Judaism becomes in the rest of one's life. Increased individual practice, when meaningful and satisfying, rarely comes at the expense of communal Jewish practice. Rather, it enhances it.

In the past, one could assume that observant Jews, steeped in communal-oriented beliefs and ritual, nevertheless had a personal sense of God. Today this assumption can no longer be made. And if one does not have a personal relationship with divinity outside the synagogue, it's not likely to exist inside either. For many, many people, wilderness is the best place to discern God's presence.

The individual nature of spiritual practice in wilderness, then, is an important corrective to the communal emphasis in Judaism, but it is neither an alternative nor a substitute. The aim is balance.

MAPPING THE HEART

DEVEKUT (CLEAVING) AND TESHUVAH (REPENTANCE)

An important dynamic of spiritual living, one that serves as an organizing principle for me, is the interplay of two classic paths to God: *devekut* and *teshuvah*.

Devekut is a spiritual term adopted by Hasidic rabbis from earlier mystics. It denotes living with the constant awareness of God's presence or being with God in an immediate sense. A derivative from the Hebrew root for "glue," *devekut* is similar to the traditional goal of the mystic: merging or entering into union with God. But in Hasidism, *devekut* is not something for exceptional moments of deep prayer or meditation. Rather, it is a state that can be maintained at all times in all endeavors by living in *mochin d'gadlut*, in expanded consciousness.

The Hasidic movement was a response to the scholastic, Talmudic culture of the late Middle Ages, an elite culture far removed from most Jews. In opposition to the stern, intellectual Judaism of their day, the Hasidim emphasized sincerity of heart over knowledge and heartfelt prayer over strict observance. They taught that one should serve God in joy and infuse prayer with dance and music. Perhaps most important, they brought mysticism to the masses by offering a new interpretation of the Kabbalah.

For the kabbalists, the action was in the godhead. Prayer and ritual were important because they affected God in the upper realms, thus bringing love and compassion into the world. They often engaged in meditation, prayer, ritual, and study in darkened rooms in the middle of the night, alone or in small groups of highly educated men. While there were some important exceptions, they generally had little use for the world beyond their books. But the Hasidim taught that the divine battlefield, as it were, is the human heart. Everyday awareness of God, by every Jew in every activity, affected God in the upper realms. The founder of Hasidim, the Ba'al Shem Tov, frequented the natural world. He taught that one could cleave to the Creator in a forest as well as a tome of Talmud. The key was *devekut*, the constant awareness of God in everything.

In the spirit of Hasidism, but in my twenty-first-century worldview, I conceive of *devekut* as Jewish mindfulness. We enter receptive mode to focus on the world around us in this moment, to be aware of the sacred in everything, to meet God in I-Thou relation. *Devekut* is a classic right-brain activity—intuitive, emotional, artistic, beyond language.

Teshuvah, on the other hand, is mostly left brain. Each of us has a personal history, a story, that constitutes the unique content of our individual selves. Particularly during the High Holy Days, we evaluate our stories by scrutinizing our past with an eye to the future. We critique our personalities. And then we employ another form of thinking that is critical to moral refinement: imagining. I envision—I image—the person I aspire to be and promise to move in that direction.[5] This left-brain activity, where we utilize language, reasoning, and imagination, is essential to personal growth. I will have more to say on *teshuvah* in chapter 13.

Devekut and *teshuvah* are opposite poles of a spectrum, the east coast and west coast of the heart. In *devekut*, we cleave to God by transcending our egos as much as possible. This path to God is intuitive, artistic, receptive, wordless, focused on the present. In practicing *teshuvah*, or repentance, we work with our egos. We try to understand our stories, probing the past, imagining the future, articulating our emotions in words, and putting our best thinking in service of *tikkun*.

A BALANCED SPIRITUAL PRACTICE

A Wild Faith places a particular emphasis on *devekut* practices—wordless spiritual exercises that focus us on the present through mindfulness and sensual awareness. This is balanced by a hefty dose of *teshuvah* practices where analysis is central. In between are practices that incorporate language and thought but eschew logic and reasoning. Rather, we direct our minds to poetry and music. This is the realm of prayer.

Why is it important to strike a balance in these paths to God?

I have a wonderful fantasy: I go into my closet, open up a drawer, and lock my ego in it for a few days. If only that were possible for all of us. We would live in a continual state of *devekut*, of receptive mode. Life would only be I-Thou, in perpetual closeness to God, full of holiness.

Unfortunately, life doesn't work that way. Since we cannot take a vacation from our personalities, we cannot change by working around them. We have to work through them. Think about what happens when people lie. They must devote their awareness to remembering the fabrication so that when the occasion arises, they remember to repeat it. Every spiritual tradition I know begins with morality, because when we move beyond the small-minded pursuits caused by jealousy, fear, and addiction and gain some calm, it is easier to see the big picture and open our hearts to God.

So we do *teshuvah*. We critique ourselves in order to identify the places we need to change. We ask forgiveness from others. We clear the clutter in our hearts and become less agitated. But of course, we can never lock our selfish traits and their vices in a closet drawer. Sometimes just identifying the cause of a bad behavior is enough, but often not. How do we actually change?

We turn to *devekut* to gain temporary respite from our fears and insecurities. We turn to *devekut* to loosen the grip of our bad habits. We turn to *devekut* to shake our hearts like a *shofar* blast.

Most of us think that we live in our minds, the place that has been (mistakenly[6]) identified by our culture as the locus of awareness. But we can transcend the realm of our fears—the (guilty) memories of the past and the (fear-filled) imaginings of the future that occupy our minds—by living in our bodies. When we focus our awareness on the present moment by dwelling in our physical senses, we get a glimpse of what life is like when we are attached to God rather than to our selves. For a moment, we have indeed locked our egos in the closet. We know that we are more than our stories.

The more time we spend in *devekut,* the more time we want to spend in *devekut.* But we also gain a new perspective with which to critique our stories and do *teshuvah.* In mindfulness, even if just for a bit, we are removed from the fears that motivate our habitual defense mechanisms. When we turn to our analytic thinking and self-critique from the place of *devekut,* we are less prone to self-deception. We are more likely to be honest and truthful about who and what we are.

So the more *devekut* I experience, the more successful my *teshuvah.* The more I do *teshuvah*—the less I am occupied by my neuroses and vices—the more I find myself in receptive mode, in *devekut.*

A wholesome spiritual practice, then, includes both these avenues. They feed each other. As we turn to the various practices of a Jewish wilderness spirituality, we gain insight into individual exercises by placing them on the *devekut/teshuvah* spectrum. This is useful as our spiritual practice matures. We can sense when our hearts need us to concentrate on *devekut* practices or when an emphasis on *teshuvah* is preferable.

6

THE MINDFUL HIKER: LEARNING TO LISTEN

In the wilderness your possessions cannot surround you. Your preconceptions cannot protect you. Your logic cannot promise you the future. Your guilt can no longer place you safely in the past. You are left alone each day with an immediacy that astonishes, chastens, and exults. You see the world as if for the first time.

Rabbi Lawrence Kushner[1]

In turning now to the specifics of a Jewish wilderness spirituality, we begin with *devekut* exercises. These practices enable us to listen deeply and directly for God by placing us firmly in the present, by leaving language behind, by opening our senses and cultivating a compassionate awareness of wild nature.

MEETING THE GOD OF SMALL THINGS

When I look back at my spiritual quest, I have no regrets but more than a little sadness. How long I looked for God in the wrong places!

So often we expect to meet God in some dramatic fashion. And since epiphanies do happen—a moment of great insight, a moment of light and love, a true meeting with another soul, an experience of overwhelming beauty—we thirst for more. But "epiphany spirituality" faces the same paradox as hedonism. The more epiphanies we have, the more we need to be satisfied. And the less likely they will happen.

In my spiritual life there were important epiphanies, but I realize now that they were strong because a new world opened up to me. I had traveled so far that everything seemed new and exotic. But this had more to do with immaturity than wisdom. As one settles into spiritual life, moments with the divine are less and less likely to carry the emotion that comes with surprise. A mature spirituality, like a long-term love, needs to find its power in the small things of everyday life. Witness the title of my teacher Jack Kornfield's recent book, *After the Ecstasy, the Laundry.*

The great teaching of Jewish mysticism, particularly important for the Hasidim, is that God is in everything. So if God is not in our field of awareness, the problem isn't with God. It's with us. I find this true and empowering. I need not strive for an elusive epiphany. I just need to open my eyes. I need to adjust my expectations and look for God in the undramatic, everyday routines of life.

This lesson came home to me on my solo wilderness retreats. Usually we entertain ourselves while hiking. Walk another mile and you get another view, and some more adrenaline from the exercise as well. That's exactly what gets taken away from you when you sit in a small circle for four days. I had to face my fears of boredom. I had to find beauty and relationship in the small, limited area that was my home.

But the payoff was enormous. I noticed patterns and textures in leaves, soil, and bark. I saw tiny spiders weave webs over the creek at dawn, from rock to rock, with amazing speed and dexterity. Rising with the day's snowmelt, the stream soon washed them away, preparing the ground for next morning's repeat performance. As I slowed down, I learned to appreciate things I never knew I had missed. It's amazing how much better you can hear when you stop to listen.

Sometimes I think of myself as a target and God as an archer with rather poor shooting skills. The archer can't hit a moving target. But when the target stands still, it's a bull's-eye every time.

While there is always an element of grace in meeting God—we never exercise complete control over these things—we need not wait for God to break through to us from the heavens. If we can change our awareness, God's presence need not be elusive and fleeting.

MAKING ROOM FOR GOD

To dwell in *devekut* consciousness—to hold God's presence in the forefront of our awareness—requires that we transcend our very selves. Like everyone else, I have a story, the stuff of my personality. There you will find my best traits and most noble virtues. But it is also the repository of my bitterness, pettiness, neurosis, and arrogance—all the things that blind me to God. *Devekut* is possible when we lessen the hold of past and future on our minds by entering receptive mode. In "emptying out," we create a space to hold awareness of the Thou. We become the empty vessel that God's spirit might fill. Moving beyond our stories is not only psychologically liberating. The practice of *devekut* actually makes room for God.

"Spirituality" is an overused and abused term these days. It carries very different meanings for different people. So let me clarify my own understanding. If I had to choose a definition for spirituality, it would be "deep listening."

The method is mindfulness. We try to live fully in the present. The people who emphasized the concept of *devekut*, the Hasidim, are famous for introducing a new practice into Jewish life that continues in our day: the singing of a *nigun*, a wordless melody of *la*s and *li*s and *oy*s. Why is it so powerful? Music fully engages the body, the center of our awareness when in receptive mode (more on body awareness in chapter 11). But more important, a *nigun* is a simple repetitive melody that functions like a mantra. It weakens the hold of the thinking mind on our awareness. Free of thoughts about past and future, we can fully focus on the world. This is the goal of every mindfulness practice. While we never fully transcend our "I," our egos, we listen more deeply with less preconception and prejudice. Our minds join our hearts as vessels that the *shefa* can fill when we live in receptive mode and invite moments of I-Thou.

THE GIFT OF WILDERNESS

Mindfulness came easily when I played football in high school. If my mind was distracted, I quickly found myself on the ground with a macro-view of the grass. It paid to pay attention. The same is true in wilderness. There are serious consequences for getting lost in the to-do list back home. When we are far from hospitals, awareness of the potential dangers in the natural world keeps us focused and alert in the present moment. Mindfulness is the great gift of wilderness.

Of course, our minds will wander at times even in wilderness. It is amazing how little people see of the world around them when walking quickly down a trail. But we can choose to walk in ways that increase our mindfulness. The practices in this chapter help us to slow down, stay present, and listen.

PRACTICES

As we turn now to specific practices in wilderness, it is important to note what is not in this book. *A Wild Faith* cannot cover safety procedures, which vary from place to place, season to season, and activity to activity. **It is your responsibility to learn and follow the appropriate safety procedures in wilderness.**

WALK SILENTLY

When I am leading a group, I start out on the trail and people follow. Inevitably, I hear the steady hum of conversation behind me. Often, someone asks a question about the flora, the geology, or lunch. Then we stop and I point out that we have been doing what every group does when left to its own devices. We talk. We are social creatures. Ignoring another person is rude, and we are often uncomfortable if we have not exchanged a least a few words with the human being standing next to us. It is the friendly thing to do.

Then I ask the group to continue in silence. Nothing we do later has quite the dramatic, paradigm-shifting effect of walking silently. When you stop thinking about what someone else is saying, or what you're saying, or what others will think of your ideas, or what you're wearing, or how you look … you get the idea. Silence frees one to focus on the natural world that we have come to experience. This is an essential practice for those who wish to be fully present in wilderness.

Practice 1
GO SILENTLY

1. As you walk (or ski or kayak) in wilderness, refrain from speech of any kind. Do not fill the silence by listening to music on your headphones.

2. If you are in a group, spread out on the trail and leave space between yourself and other hikers.

For people who have never walked quietly, the change is revolutionary. Suddenly flowers are everywhere and birdsong fills the air. Many people appear to have a paradoxical experience. The more they concentrate on outer geography, the more aware they become of inner geography—their emotions, feelings, and yearnings. In reality, it is not a contradiction at all. Free of the incessant chatter of the media, the Internet, and social niceties, awareness grows into a fullness that holds everything we experience. The more we are alert and focused on our surroundings, the more we are aware of our interaction with them. As Martin Buber showed us in relating to a tree, sometimes the deepest dialogue is wordless.

MEDITATIVE 25-25-50 WALKING

When we remove ourselves from the social world by walking silently, other distractions are ready to jump in. Our minds might occupy our attention with worries regarding tomorrow's meeting, regrets about something we said yesterday, or thoughts about what we're having for dinner. Meditation is the art of dealing with our restless minds in order to live fully in the present.

One meditative strategy is to occupy the mind with several simultaneous tasks, all focused on the present. This is my favorite way of staying in the here and now while hiking. The goal is simply to pay attention to the natural world.

Practice 2
MEDITATIVE WALKING

1. While standing still in wilderness, focus on your breath. You might listen for the subtle sound of breathing, notice the rising and falling of the belly and chest, or focus on the sensation of air passing through the nostrils. When thoughts arise, gently let them go and return to the breath.

2. After a minute, leave half your attention on the breath and place the other half on the bottoms of your feet. Feel the pressure of your body on the earth; notice the constant adjustments your muscles make to maintain balance.

3. After another minute, shift your focus once again. Place 25 percent of your awareness on your breath, another 25 percent on the soles of your feet, and 50 percent on the world around you. Begin to walk, taking in all the sounds and sights of the land you are traversing.

4. When your mind wanders and focus fades, try not to get angry at yourself. This happens to everyone, no matter how experienced at meditative walking. Gently return your attention to the breath and the soles of your feet, then look, listen, and continue on.

FOCUS ON THE SENSES

We can further focus our attention on the world around us by lending our awareness to one particular sense. As we walk (or kayak or ski), we place our conscious attention solely on sound, sight, smell, or touch.

Practice 3
SENSE WALKING

1. In a wilderness place, begin with sound. Place your attention on your faculty to hear, and listen intently for birdcalls, the rustle of your boots on dead leaves, the whistle of the wind through trees and canyons, the gurgle of a stream. What do you hear that you have never heard before? Move beyond your story by concentrating your attention on wild nature.

2. Repeat with the senses of touch, smell, and sight.

SEEING WITHOUT EYES: BLINDFOLD GAMES

Much has been written by eco-philosophers about the dominance of sight in contemporary society. We enjoy sound, touch, and taste, but unlike earlier times, we are almost completely dependent on sight to succeed in the world. These exercises activate the other senses and show us how much richer is our perception of the natural world when we use them.

These simple exercises require a bandana and a friend. They were developed by innovative master nature educator Joseph Cornell.[2]

PICTURE FRAMES

1. Working in pairs, one person is the camera, the other the photographer. The photographer blindfolds the camera and carefully leads the camera to a particular scene of the photographer's choosing. It might be a grand vista or an acorn on the ground. The camera may be guided by the photographer to look up or kneel as needed. The photographer adjusts the camera by shifting his or her head into the correct position.

2. The camera, without moving his or her head, removes the blindfold for five seconds. (If you took your glasses off to put on the blindfold, put them back on.) It is helpful if the photographer alerts the camera beforehand: this is a wide-angle shot, this is a close-up. Replace the blindfold and move on to the next shot.

3. Do three to six photos, and switch roles.

How does it feel to see from a viewpoint that someone else has chosen? Did you see things that, if left to your own devices, you would have missed? Discuss with your partner.

MEET A TREE

1. Find a spot amidst a number of similar-sized trees. Again working in pairs, the sighted partner spins the blindfolded one around and around until the person loses his or her sense of direction.

2. The sighted partner leads the blind one to a tree, where he or she spends a few minutes getting to know the tree by touching and grasping it.

3. Return to the starting spot, where again the sighted partner spins the blindfolded one around.

4. The blindfold is removed, and the person tries to find his or her tree.

I once did this exercise with schoolchildren on the grounds of their synagogue. (Congregation Bet Haverim in Davis, California, is blessed with a redwood grove in the heart of their campus!) At pickup time, several students were seen gesturing before their parents, "Look, this is my tree."

The following exercise is the same as Sense Walking (practice 3), only now we heighten the other senses by eliminating sight.

Practice 6
BLIND SENSE WALKING

1. Sound: The sighted partner slowly leads the blindfolded one down the trail. The blind partner concentrates on hearing. This exercise can also be done by oneself by staying in one spot. Simply blindfold yourself and listen. Try it at the beach.

2. Touch: The blindfolded partner is slowly brought down a trail by the sighted partner, focusing on the feel of his or her feet against the ground and the wind against the skin. The leader stops occasionally to direct the hands of the blind partner to an object: a rock, branch, leaf, etc. Be sure that the groping of the blind partner will not injure the object (such as a cocoon). **Avoid thorns, and be sure to know poison oak and other irritants.**

THE WIDER VIEW

The way we twenty-first-century Westerners view the world is quite new and different, not figuratively, but actually. Much of what we see requires narrow vision. Our eyes are directed to images in narrow places: billboards, computer monitors, TV screens, books, and newspapers. We read small specific images, the letters of the alphabet, most everywhere we turn. In order to function in our society, we develop tunnel vision.

For most of history, humans needed to notice movement to avoid predators and hunt successfully, especially on the periphery. Western colonialists commented on the "shifty-eyed" native who would not look them in the eye for more than a second. Of course, the natives were simply employing the gaze that best suited their needs. In nature, we are often served better by wide-angle rather than narrow vision. We simply see more. We receive more.

Practice 7
WIDE-ANGLE VISION

Walking slowly, let your vision soften. Try to take in everything around you. Notice what is on the periphery without moving your head. Avoid shifting your narrow focus from one object to the next. Rather, keep your gaze steady and try to expand the range of things you are seeing and noticing at the same time.

BE SAFE

Safety in the wilderness is a matter of mindfulness. Grizzly bears and rattlesnakes are awareness animals. Poison oak is an awareness plant. If we do not pay attention to them, we suffer.

Practice 8
BE ESPECIALLY MINDFUL OF SAFETY ISSUES AND PROCEDURES

Know the potential dangers wherever you go in wilderness. Pay special attention to avoiding them.

Since everyone has to steer clear of danger, it seems superfluous to mention this as a practice, but it is important to note. It is the reason that mindfulness comes naturally in wilderness.

In addition to the healthy fear and respect we lend these "awareness" plants and animals (as well as river currents, avalanche fields, weather systems, etc.), we can be grateful to them for keeping us in the present.

INTRODUCING THE SOUL-O SITE

Solitary time in a natural setting for spiritual purposes is almost as old as recorded history. Witness Moses, Jesus, Buddha, and Mohammed. Most Native American cultures sent their male adolescents on vision quests to mark and induce the transition to adulthood. The young boy would spend four days in a small circle, often a pit, praying for a vision while fasting from food and water.

The Hasidic leader Rabbi Nachman of Breslov made a practice of talking to God while walking alone in the forests of eastern Europe. I doubt the leaders of Outward Bound had heard of him when they began to send participants on "solo" periods during their innovative trips. Somewhere along the line, an obvious connection was made, and "solo" received a more appropriate spelling: "Soul-O."

A Soul-O site is the place a person chooses to spend time alone in wilderness. Ideally, one returns to the same place repeatedly over time, perhaps a spot by the river on your favorite hike. Or, inspired by the Native American rite, one spends a day, or as many as four, in the same small circle.

The beauty of the natural world is often overwhelming. Enraptured, we stand in awe. But we easily become spoiled. We crave another, better view (just over the next ridge, isn't it?). We hope that tonight's sunset will outdo the previous one. While it is certainly acceptable to pursue the beautiful, we run the risk of holding nature like a museum. We judge the elements of the landscape against each other for their artistic merit. Rather than an I-Thou relationship with nature, we become judgmental critics.

In a Soul-O site, there is no switching to another channel for more entertainment by hiking on until another vista comes into view, no skiing a new run for the adrenaline rush, no climbing another rock face so that one might brag about it around the campfire. Instead, we are invited to explore the awesome mystery of the things that we are usually moving too fast to see: a cocoon on the underside of a twig, the pattern of a leaf, the difference between two blades of grass. The beauty is subtle, and while we still crave to see something new, the drive for entertainment gives way to curiosity. We acquire a profound respect for the plants and animals we come to know intimately during our Soul-O time.

Practice 9
FIND YOUR SOUL-O SITE

1. Choose a Soul-O site by listening to the landscape. When you feel drawn to a particular place, check it out. If your body feels relaxed, spend some time in the place. You might perform a four winds ceremony (see practice 35) or a gratitude exercise (see practice 14).

2. If you are tense or troubled or your mind begins to race, keep looking. But realize that you must first be calm and relaxed to listen well. Some people obsess over sites and never find the "right" one. This is more a statement about their neurotic mind than the area around them. Most places in the natural world will be fruitful as a Soul-O site.

3. **Use common sense.** If you will need to refill your water bottle, choose a place close to water. Do not choose a Soul-O spot next to ants; be aware of high season for no-see-ums and mosquitoes; make sure you have shade in the desert, protection from weather in the mountains; take adequate food, water, and clothing. The right equipment can make a big difference, and not only during a storm. A backpacker's chair, meditation cushion, or non-rubber Yoga mat might prove useful.

Soul-O site practice is powerful. We don't just stop to smell the roses. We learn more about the sense of smell and the beauty of roses than we could possibly have imagined. Most of the exercises in *A Wild Faith* are doable in a Soul-O spot. The following mindfulness practices are well suited for Soul-O site practice.

STOP AND LISTEN

I always assumed that hunters track their prey. I was thoroughly surprised when I observed my cousin on a hunting trip. He "took a stand" behind some trees and waited quietly for a deer to walk by! (None did.)

Joseph Cornell notes that this technique works for photographers and spiritual seekers as well. After you settle down, the life in the area will gradually return to the rhythm it enjoyed before you kicked up a ruckus by moving in. Bird life will resume almost immediately. And after a few minutes, minor and sometimes not so minor animal life will saunter by as if you were not there.

Practice 10
TAKE A STAND

1. Choose a place, perhaps a Soul-O site. **Use the same common sense: avoid ants, find a balance of sun and shade, and so on.** To view larger animals, try locating yourself upwind and close to a water source. Your chances are better if you are there when the animals are active, at dawn and dusk.

2. Lie down or sit in a comfortable position, and be still.

Over the years I've had close encounters with all kinds of wildlife. On my first solo wilderness retreat, I camped across from a dead tree. Every day at sunset, an immature bald eagle perched on it to call out for his friends. (Birds often prefer to chirp for their companions on dead trees, as they are trying to be seen.)

While engaged in many of the exercises in this book, such as praying, writing, or sketching, if you keep quiet and still, you will also be "taking a stand."

JOSEPH CORNELL'S QUIET THE MIND EXERCISES

In *Listening to Nature*, Joseph Cornell presents a striking image to describe what happens when we become still and present while observing nature. Picture your mind as the surface of an alpine lake and your thoughts the wind. When the mind is turbulent, the wind sends ripples along the lake's surface and nothing is reflected. When the mind is calm, the wind still, the lake reflects the landscape on the other side with perfect clarity. We see what lies before our eyes.

Cornell offers the simplest of sitting meditations for the purpose of relaxing our minds and achieving the clarity of vision that mindfulness brings. Here are his instructions for meditating while viewing the beauty of wilderness.

Practice 11
SIMPLE MEDITATION

First, relax the body. Do this by inhaling and tensing all over: feet, legs, back, arms, neck, face—as much as you possibly can. Then throw the breath out and relax completely. Repeat this several times.

To practice the technique itself: observe the natural flow of your breath. Do not control the breath in any way! Simply follow it with your attention. Each time you inhale, think "Still." Each time you exhale, think "Ness." Repeating "Still ... Ness" with each complete breath helps focus the mind and prevents your attention from wandering from the present moment.

During the pauses between inhalation and exhalation, stay in the present moment, calmly observing whatever is in front of you. If thoughts of the past or future disturb your mind, just calmly, patiently bring your attention back to what is before you, and to repeating "Still ... Ness" with your breathing.[3]

Even when we stop to admire a spectacular view, the mind wanders. But just as in walking meditation, we can consciously bring our awareness back to the natural world.

Practice 12
QUIET THE MIND

1. When sitting or standing in one place, practice simple meditation to stay focused on the natural world.

2. Find or compose a prayer to quiet the mind.

3. Recite it when you realize that your mind has wandered, bringing your attention back to the natural world.

4. Memorize the prayer so that you can respond immediately in a moment of need.

Cornell composed this prayer to help calm the mind:

> Let my mind become silent,
> And my thoughts come to rest.
> I want to see
> All that is before me.
> In self-forgetfulness,
> I become everything.[4]

If you like, you can compose other lines that work better for you. The trick is to memorize them so that when the moment of revelation arrives, when you realize that your mind has wandered, you can gently recite your poem and return awareness to the natural world.

LET IT BE

My vision quest teacher, John Milton, instructed us to avoid disturbing the "rock people." He gave us the following instruction.

Practice 13
DISTURB NOTHING

1. Notice where you place your feet at all times.

2. If you move a pebble or a rock, put it back.

It is virtually impossible not to disturb a stone in rocky terrain, so at first I found the exercise quite maddening. Remarkably, within a day, I was able to go hours without moving a pebble as I scooted around camp. Paying attention to precisely where we place our feet is a great art, one that primitive hunters must develop to stalk their prey.

TRACKING

While I cannot teach them in this book, other activities that increase mindfulness in wilderness bear mentioning.

Tracking is a superb way to pay close attention to the natural world. Trackers scour the landscape for signs of wildlife. To interpret what they see, they learn not only the physiology and habitual behaviors of animals, but also the soils and flora of the biosphere, as these predict the presence of wildlife. Tracking is a highly valuable skill well worth the time to learn.

While there are many books on the subject, it is best to begin by studying with a teacher. I also advise beginning in the winter. Animal tracks are easy to spot and identify in the snow.

And if you are so inclined, tracking leads to some excellent shots ... with your camera.

DRAWING AND MINDFUL PHOTOGRAPHY

Drawing requires deep attention to the detail and nuance of the natural world. While one can obsess about the product rather than enjoy the process, sketching is an excellent way to dwell in nature rather than one's self. You can't help but notice disparate shapes, subtle patterns, and varieties of color that you would have missed otherwise.

Simple pencils will do. I can attest that no previous experience is necessary, just a pencil and a blank page. Remember, it is what you see and learn that counts, not the drawing. (See Hannah Hinchman's contemporary classic, *A Trail Through Leaves: The Journal as a Path to Place*[5] for more guidance.)

The same can be said of photography, though here the danger of caring more about the photograph than the photographee can lead to an exploitive relationship with the natural world, not to mention annoying anyone else around you. However, great photographers are led by the camera to see so much more than they would have otherwise. Mindful photography can lead to immersion in wild nature rather than alienation from it.

Many practices in other chapters are also effective in quieting the mind and directing our full attention to what lies before us. In particular, chant is an excellent mindfulness practice (see practice 27).

What makes a spiritual practice in wilderness different is that it *is* in wilderness. Mindfulness is the foundation for the practices that follow in *A Wild Faith,* and not only because focusing awareness on the world makes room for God by helping us beyond our stories. Rather, through mindfulness, we truly connect to the wild places that our eyes behold and our feet caress.

YEARNING AND GRATITUDE: OPENING THE HEART TO GOD

Imagine if at every moment we each embraced the world as the gift it is: An apple is a gift; the color pink is a gift; the blue sky is a gift; the scent of honeysuckle is a gift.... We are called not merely to notice casually now and then that something is special and nice but to sustain and deepen a profound and sustained gratitude. Indeed, the more we acknowledge our gratefulness, the more we temper our tendency to be users, despoilers, arrogant occupiers.

We are on the way to *kedusha*.

Rabbi Marcia Prager[1]

What is an open heart? Author M. J. Ryan offers this insightful observation: openheartedness is "living in the spirit of joyful expectation."[2] We have an intention to remain alert and unshielded, happily looking forward to what life will offer. We cannot control the outcome of our meetings with our fellow sojourners on earth or with God. But instead of fearing the unknown, we try to live with hearts open and minds free. We try to be the kind of person who "joyfully expects" to see the sacred in others.

This is another way of stating our desire to live in receptive mode with an eye to I-Thou encounter. While the goal remains "deep listening," however, the methods presented in this chapter are quite different. In pure mindfulness practices, we reach out by emptying out. Here, we use our mind to set an intention. We cultivate our heart's desire by giving it voice. We speak our "joyful expectation" to see the sacred in the world, inviting God's presence into our lives.

THE POWER OF INTENTION

Without exception, my spiritual teachers insist on the importance of articulating, affirming, and reaffirming one's intention when engaging in spiritual practice. Intention gives direction to our thoughts and actions; it helps us to garner concentration and discipline.

Intention-setting is another one of the paradoxes of spiritual living. For spiritual practice to succeed, we need to let go of undue judgment and expectations. As much as possible, we need to give our egos a rest. But it takes willpower to stick with spiritual practice. The usual external motivations, such as social approval or financial gain, do not apply. Rather, it takes a strong ego—an ego whose strength comes from surrender to the heart and yearning for the sacred.[3]

YEARNING

At the foundation of spiritual living is the basic desire to increase the love and holiness in our lives. We consciously recognize that we want to grow and mature.

Yearning in a spiritual context is "holy desire." Not everyone has it, but I think most of us do. We long for purpose and meaning. We yearn to become better people and live better lives. We want to love with all our heart and connect with all that is holy and sacred in this world. Deep down, we know that everything depends on how this unfathomable, mysterious drive plays out in our lives.

All of us face the hedonist paradox. The more we have, the more we want, but the more we get, the less satisfied we feel. On the other hand, the more we give, the greater our happiness. The joy of love knows no limits. Yearning is the beginning of the way out of the hedonist's dilemma. We express our holy desire to lead a life filled with love, response-ability, and service.

A LANGUAGE OF THE HEART

If *devekut* practices are about bypassing language, and *teshuvah* practices employ analytical thought, a majority of the practices in *A Wild Faith* fall into that middle ground where we put words in the service of the heart. In yearning and gratitude practices, we connect to our heart's desire and give it voice. Even though we use language (left brain), we try to stay with our feelings, emotions, and intuitions (right brain). We do so by turning to poetic rather than analytic thought, to words embedded in concrete situations rather than abstract ideas. We turn from word-logic to word-play and word-artistry.

It's not easy. There is a reason that great poets and liturgists are few and far between. Attempts to describe that which is essentially beyond description usually fall short. Worse, spiritual practice is not a spectator sport. To put my holy desire into words, I ought to compose my own prayers. One of those great word artists ought to be me! But how can I put yearning into words without embarrassing myself?

I wish there was an easy answer, like taking a poetry workshop or swallowing a creativity pill. If only that were possible. So what to do? Frankly, we just have to get over it. We should not let the inadequacy of our own words deter us from composing poems and prayers. Their importance is in expressing what is actually going on in *our* hearts in *this* moment. Even Shakespeare can't do this for us. The strength of our words comes from the emotion we put into them. What they lack in artistry is more than made up for by sincerity, honesty, and desire.

Finally, in setting intention and expressing desire in language, it is helpful to speak out loud. In bringing words to breath, in speaking and hearing them, we make language an immediate, bodily experience. The Rabbis understood the great difference between the written word and the spoken word. Even during the silent prayer in the Jewish prayer service, the *Amidah*, one is enjoined to speak one's prayers in a whisper. Words spoken take on a reality that they cannot attain on the printed page.

EXPERIENCE GRATITUDE

When I finished Israeli desert guide school, I guided American teenagers visiting Israel in the desert mountains near Eilat. The summer temperatures often ran over a hundred degrees. But unlike the other groups that stayed in air-conditioned hostels, we in the Reform Movement and Kibbutz Yahel, Israel's first Reform kibbutz, camped in wilderness. We spent as much time as possible in the natural world. In order to make it work, we woke the campers before dawn and hiked early. We went swimming at the beach during the heat of the day and resumed hiking in the late afternoon. It worked beautifully. But we didn't start dinner until after dark, after which the exhausted kids (and guide) fell asleep. By the third morning, after two nights of sleep that really added up to only one, the usually exuberant teenagers had scowls on their faces as we began our 6 a.m. hike. They moved slowly and looked at me with rather sincere malice.

There, at the northern end of the Sinai desert, I thought to myself, "So this is what Moses had to deal with."

I soon found a way to remedy the situation. After a quarter of a mile on the trail, I would stop the group and ask, "What do you have to complain about?" At first they wouldn't think I was serious, but with a little convincing, they would let loose. The teenagers thought of five or six things that made them the most justifiably miserable people in the world.

After they ran out of complaints, I asked, "What do you have to be grateful for?" I stopped the list at ten or so. It could have gone on forever. Even in their despair, the campers' faces lit up and their voices gained more and more enthusiasm as they thought of all the things for which they were thankful. They returned to themselves and hiked with their usual joy.

The "attitude of gratitude" is probably cliché by now, but like most spiritual truisms, it is based on something real and enduring. In my opinion there is no more powerful way of changing our mood and opening the heart than simply saying "thanks."

M. J. Ryan explains the dynamics of living in gratitude:[4]

- It is impossible to experience gratitude when your heart is closed. Rather, it immediately opens us up to the beauty of the moment, welcoming rather than fearing the unexpected.

- Our hearts may experience many emotions, but for the most part, we can only do one at a time. Gratitude is the antidote to fear, bitterness, and anger.

- The more grateful you are, the easier it is to give and the more you love.

- Gratitude is like a flashlight in the dark. We don't always see the good and the sacred, even though they are always there. When we shine the light of gratitude on the world, we see the basic goodness of God's creation.[5]

- When we are grateful, we feel connected to that for which we are grateful. Whereas depression fosters tunnel vision, saying thanks directs our attention toward the big picture. Gratitude makes us feel at home in the world.

Gratitude is the elixir of spiritual practice.

PRACTICES

PSALMS AND TRADITIONAL PRAYERS
Saying thanks to God directly through prayer is the most basic gratitude practice in Judaism.

Traditional prayers and blessings are full of nature imagery. They express gratitude to God for the grandeur of nature and praise the natural world for its beauty and connection to God. Saying them *in* nature, alternating one's gaze between book and wilderness, gives poetic voice to the yearning in our hearts.

One of the very first prayers in the morning service is a blessing thanking God for … the rooster. Really. The prayer gives thanks for the rooster's ability to differentiate between day and night. Before alarm clocks, those who needed to take advantage of every drop of daylight, particularly farmers, benefited greatly from this animal's uncanny ability to wake us up just as the stars begin to fade.

Saying thanks to the rooster, of course, is the equivalent of starting your day by jumping out of bed and thanking God for your alarm clock! It's not the natural thing to do. But through prayer, Jewish ritual immediately moves us into a place of gratitude. We start the day seeing the cup half-full. More on the traditional prayers is found in chapters 8 and 10.

SAYING THANKS
The easiest way to express gratitude is to speak it. It is probably the most effective way as well. Giving voice to a thought grounds it in our bodies and concretizes our sentiments.

One can say thanks directly to the various entities we encounter in nature, marking God's role in facilitating this incredible planet and, if you are a mystic, remembering that each is made of god-stuff and channels the *shefa*, the divine vitality and intelligence flowing through the earth. Like praying for people in need of healing, the simplicity of this practice makes it easy to gloss over its powerful effect on us, not to mention the beings we are thanking.

Practice 14
SAY THANKS TO THE NATURAL WORLD

1. Approach a stone, plant, or creature and direct your full attention toward it. You might take a moment to appreciate its beauty before speaking.

2. Say thanks, using your own words. "Thank you, flower, for the joy you bring me." To an old tree one might say, "Thank you, grandmother, for your shade and for sheltering my tent from the wind." Just saying "thanks" with sincerity is enough.

3. I often touch the plant or stone while speaking to it.

One can say thanks anywhere, anytime, but I give this practice priority before I settle into a campsite or, more important, a Soul-O site.

There is no getting around it: in Western cultures this just seems crazy. According to modern science, nature is a machine, and this practice is a waste of time. To do it probably requires overcoming considerable internal resistance. But why let others decide? I hope you'll check it out for yourself. (Appendix 2 deals with this subject.)

WORKING WITH PSALMS

I think of psalms as "yearning poems," that particular kind of poetry where insight is fused with desire for one's beloved. Not everyone identifies with the theology of the writers, but for those who do, the psalms continue to move us, especially if we know Hebrew. They have stood the test of time. The artistry of the authors reflects the beauty of the natural world. As they were written to be spoken rather than read, be sure to recite them out loud.

RECITE A PSALM

1. Recite a psalm in wilderness.

2. Psalms with nature imagery include 19, 29, 95–99, 104, 147, and 148.

3. Recite a psalm you have memorized.

For a variation on this exercise, see practice 23, "Carry a Power *Pasuk.*"

BE A CONTEMPORARY PSALMIST
Creative writing in wilderness, particularly poetry, is a unique way of letting the heart express its deepest yearnings. It draws out and gives shape to those strong but often inchoate emotions that the sacred elicits in moments of I-Thou.

Psalms often employ descriptive, third-person language.

> The voice of Adonai is over the waters;
>> the God of glory thunders,
>> Adonai, over the mighty waters.
> The voice of Adonai is power;
>> the voice of Adonai is majesty;
>> the voice of Adonai breaks cedars;
>> Adonai shatters the cedars of Lebanon.
>> (Psalm 29:3–5)

But psalms often turn to second-person language, and herein lies their power as poems of yearning. The psalmist speaks directly to God, the world, or other people, expressing his or her raw emotions.

> Answer us with victory through awesome deeds,
>> O God, our deliverer,
>> in whom all the ends of the earth
>> and the distant seas
>> put their trust. (Psalm 65:6)
> O God, my King from of old,
>> who brings deliverance throughout the land;
>> it was You who drove back the sea with Your might …
>> it was You who released springs and torrents,
>> who made mighty rivers run dry;
>> the day is Yours, the night also;
>> it was You who set in place the orb of the sun;
>> You fixed all the boundaries of the earth;
>> summer and winter—You made them
>>> (Psalm 74:12–13, 15–17)

There is a great deal of wonderful nature poetry that most of us would consider "spiritual." Psalms differ, however, in their emphasis on God's relation to the universe and its inhabitants. The same is true of contemporary psalms, of contemporary poems. They deal openly with spiritual issues, even if they don't mention God specifically.

The contemporary psalmists, the modern poets, who move me most also use second-person language. It helps to read them to see how we might express our own emotions in wilderness. (See practice 17 and Resources for a list of my favorites.) However, while it is inspiring, and therefore important, to read a great poet, it is also intimidating. How can we ever measure up? The point to remember is that we don't have to. The goal is to speak our feelings and to articulate our own truth. We're not out to win poetry awards. Rather, we hope to express our yearnings as honestly as possible.[6]

Practice 16
WRITE A PSALM

1. In your journal, write a poem that expresses your yearning.

2. Try to use second-person language in at least some of the poem.

3. Read it out loud in the place that inspired your writing.

KEEPING A JOURNAL

A journal is an essential tool in spiritual practice. It can be put to use in creative writing exercises such as "Writing a Psalm." Journaling is critical in *teshuvah* practices, where we attempt to unravel the mystery of our psyches, in part, by employing our best thinking. Writing helps us to clarify our thoughts and figure things out. And it's nice, of course, to write down where we have been and what we have done, so that we can remember later. I always carry a journal, which sometimes doubles as a sketchbook.

But there is a tension between pure listening practices, where we refrain from using words at all, and those spiritual exercises where we employ language. The danger is that by constantly writing in a journal, we spend too much time in our heads and too little time in our hearts and bodies. And since we Westerners live mostly in our heads and find mindfulness difficult, it is a strong temptation indeed.

Mindfulness practice often clears the clutter in our minds, allowing "deeper" insights to arise. This is good. But since this deep insight will surely change my life, how can I just let it go? I want to write it down and think about it right away. And so I am seduced into analytical thought. But thinking is also a way for the ego to regain control by taking us out of receptive mode.

So what should one do when the thought of the century arises during walking meditation or another mindfulness practice?

First, if it is truly important, know that it will come back to you. And if it is not important, then good riddance. So don't worry about it. By the way, I have found that many a revolutionary insight turns out to be quite ordinary twenty-four hours later. Since our egos are more secure when our awareness is occupied by our thinking minds, we have a tendency to misjudge these things in the excitement of the moment.

Second, you can do mindfulness practices and journal about them later. In fact, journaling is an excellent way to transition from wilderness retreat to everyday life. We have a chance to think about what we learned through mindfulness and how to integrate it into our lives. And of course, we might simply want to record the events of our practice in order to remember them in a year or two.

If you are nevertheless concerned that you will forget something important, or that you will have difficulty reconstructing what you did during your wilderness retreat, there is a simple solution. Write a word or two in your journal to jog your memory later. I actually mean *a* word or *two*. If it is important, that is all it will take to remember it well. We tend to recall what we learn in receptive mode quite easily.

When I hike, the more I have to carry on my back, the smaller my journal. Journals with waterproof pages are quite nice, but also quite heavy. A self-closing plastic bag is generally enough to keep your journal dry.

READ A CONTEMPORARY PSALM

Many contemporary poets reflect the same passion and heart stirring that moved the ancient authors of the psalms. Wilderness, where transcendence is so palpable, provides the perfect context to receive and grapple with the spirit of a gifted author.

You might consider memorizing a poem that has moved you. Offering it out loud at an appropriate moment in wilderness with the emphasis and articulation that memorization allows can be mesmerizing both to you as well as your companions.[7]

Practice 17
RECITE A POEM

1. Bring your favorite spiritual poems with you into wilderness.

2. Read or, preferably, recite a poem in wilderness.

3. Memorize your favorite poems; recite them at appropriate moments.

I rarely venture into wilderness without Rainer Maria Rilke's *Book of Hours*. Other favorite poets include Rumi, Mary Oliver, and David Whyte (see Resources).

Many practices in coming chapters also express yearning and gratitude. Chant is a particularly effective yearning and gratitude practice (see practice 27).

8

SEEING THE SACRED:
THE WAY OF BLESSING
PART I

Each moment offers us more gifts than we imagine.
We wake up and are alive; we have miraculous bodies;
we are free; we have minds that learn and hearts that
love. We can taste and feel. Our lives are a banquet of
sensations. Take a moment and remember: the tang of
tangerine, the sensuous sweetness of milk chocolate,
spicy cinnamon tea, hearty whole-grain bread, biscuits
dripping butter and honey, pasta with parmesan and
garlic, cold watermelon on a hot summer day....
Hidden wonders lie even in the most mundane tasks of
our lives, from washing dishes in slithery suds to pink
baby-bottoms at diaper-change time. When we want
to acknowledge the miracle of these moments, to
remember them, to log them, we can do this with a
brakha [blessing].

Rabbi Marcia Prager[1]

"All the people saw the thunder" on Mount Sinai, reads the Book
of Exodus (20:15).

But shouldn't one *hear* thunder? ask the biblical commentators. To me, the best explanation is that seeing is not just about
sight. It's about vision. It's about everything that informs our

sight—our touching and hearing, our personal experiences and family history. It's about our worldview, the comprehensive way in which we see the world.

THE AMBIGUITY OF VISION

Vision is a notoriously fickle enterprise. Two people eye a cow. One sees a sacred animal that must be protected; the other sees next week's lunch. Beyond simple perceptions such as the color of a car, what we see is profoundly affected by what we have seen, heard, touched, learned, thought, felt, and experienced in life.

Vision is partly subjective because our brains are wired to see the world through concepts. Once I've learned what a mountain is, I can't see another one without identifying it, consciously or unconsciously, as a mountain. Once I've learned what a table is, I can't help but see a table when I look at one, even if it has three legs.

This is the great blessing and curse of being human. By manipulating the conceptual beliefs operating on our psyches— that is, through education—we shape how we see the world. Not just how we *think* about it, but how we *see* it. For example, let's assume that sometime early in your life, when you were learning how to speak, your parents took you to a zoo or farm. They showed you a beautiful majestic animal and told you that it was a horse. You were thrilled. But then they told you something highly counterintuitive, if not downright ridiculous. The plastic toy in your bathtub was … a horse!

Your parents were not crazy. They were teaching you what you need to know, how you need to see, to get on in life.

CULTURE AND SIGHT

The world doesn't just happen to appear to us the way it does. Our cultures and subcultures teach us the "right" way to see, and we learn the "correct" beliefs to do so. These concepts arm us with the vision we need to succeed in life, and that varies with the demands of the environment. For most of human history, children were taught how to read weather, avoid predators, and identify edible plants. We learn how to ride subways, program VCRs, work around computer programming glitches, and order grande decaf dry vanilla cappuccinos. We learn the speech and unwritten dress code of our schools and workplaces, what is expected of a friend, and what makes one a good parent. Some concepts we learn explicitly in school, but most are passed on through song, story, and deed by adults, older siblings, and in our day, the media. As my ten-year-old nephew says, "Everything I need to know I learned from cartoons."

It's amazing how powerful this simple truth is. Witness our politics, where "spin" and "framing" are the buzzwords of the day. An environmentalist laments a "clear-cut" forest, while a timber industry representative speaks of a "harvest." But this is much more than clever wordplay. Words reflect the beliefs that shape our guts. Most of the world loves to eat pork. Yet I know observant Jews, raised in a culture where pigs represent defilement, who become nauseated at the sight of pork. Our concepts of what is morally acceptable inform our senses. They become part of us on a deep, subconscious level.

I am walking down the street, late for an appointment, when I see an elderly man who needs help crossing the street. I avert my eyes and hurry on. That night, I think about the man, and I feel terrible. I saw the need in his eyes, and I should have helped him. My parents and teachers taught me to behave differently. When I think about it, I know what's right. The next day, I am in the same situation and think to myself, "Aha, this time, I'll help." And I do. The next day, too. The following week, when I am confronted again with the same situation, I don't think at all. I immediately help the man. A learned piece of cultural information becomes an attitude, a highly emotional "gut" reaction, an intuitive part of my most basic self.

LEARNING TO SEE THE SACRED

Reality, then, is terribly subjective and contentious. One person perceives the redwood tree as a sacred life, another as the backyard deck. That's the bad news. But there is good news here, too. We humans have an extraordinary capacity to change the way we experience the world. We can choose to see the cup half-full. In moments of awe, the transcendent breaks through and we see the sacred. Now that we know what to look for, we can choose to see holiness in the world every day.

It's not necessarily easy. If you were raised in a Western country, you have likely internalized the prejudices of a culture dominated by the beliefs that make science and technology possible. The only truths we can trust are truths proved by scientific method; they pertain only to material things that can be measured. Nature is a "resource"; plants and nonreasoning animals have no value other than their use to humans. Divinity, if it exists at all, is hidden from the physical realm.

Educating ourselves to see *kedushah*, holiness, is easier said than done.

Difficult, however, does not mean impossible. Our culture has taught us to see nature as an impersonal machine, but you are probably reading this book, despite what you learned, because you sense the sacred in wilderness. If we are open, every new experience challenges our existing beliefs. Moreover, we can educate ourselves with the principles and ideas of our best thinking. We need not be victims of our upbringing.

Of the many tools Judaism brings to the task of shaping our vision, perhaps none is as powerful as the simple act of saying a blessing.

THE POWER OF BLESSINGS

What happens when we say a blessing with intention and awareness? Let's take a common example, the blessing over bread.

> *Baruch atah Adonai Eloheinu Melech ha'olam, hamotzi lechem min ha'aretz.*
> Praised be You Adonai, our God, Sovereign of the universe, who brings forth bread from the earth.

Reciting the blessing, I immediately move from what Hasidic teachers call *mochin d'katnut* (small mind) to *mochin d'gadlut* (expansive mind). I am brought out of everyday awareness, where attention to the petty details can lead to pettiness, to the big-picture view that recognizes a potential moment of holiness in every thing and every act. I express my gratitude, remembering the miracle of plant life and the grace of having food to eat at all when so many people do not.

Of course, I can dispassionately say the blessing by rote. But if I allow the words to affect me, if I enter "blessing consciousness," I see an entirely different world. There is no room in my awareness for the anger I was feeling toward a business associate, no need for the frustration with myself I was carrying a moment ago. This is a time to welcome *chesed* (grace; loving-kindness) and say thanks for the great fortune that is mine.

The world that makes me mad and the world that fills me with awe and joy are both there. But emotionally, I can only see one at a time. When I say a blessing, I am making a choice to recognize that the cup is half-full. I am choosing to *see*—to sense, feel, and envision—a world filled with holiness.[2]

Whether hiking a trail or sniffing wildflowers or retreating from a storm, there is hardly a time where one cannot find an appropriate blessing from the tradition.

Practice 18
WILDERNESS BLESSINGS

1. Study the list of traditional blessings beginning on page 197 and carry them with you in wilderness.

2. Memorize as many as possible.

3. Where appropriate, recite them. The closer the recitation to the act of seeing or smelling, the better.

These blessings have been culled from Jewish tradition, mostly from the Talmud, and are found in many prayer books. For the practice to be effective, it is best to memorize nature blessings. We may not always have a prayer book handy to look up the appropriate blessing. More important, the blessing is meant to influence our reaction to the natural world when we experience it, not minutes or even seconds later.

RESPONSE BLESSINGS

Most Jewish blessings are said before the act in order to set an intention. We bless wine before we drink, bread before we eat. We say the Torah study blessing before we study.

But nature blessings come *after* the act. We hear thunder, see the ocean, or smell a flower and then speak the words of the blessing. The blessing is a *response* to an unexpected, spontaneous perception. It's not scheduled for before dinner or when the sun sets on Friday.

"Reaction" or "response" blessings put us in a seemingly paradoxical situation. How can I program a spontaneous reaction? And why should I try? Didn't Martin Buber teach that once you become aware of yourself experiencing an I-Thou encounter, it's already I-It?

Certainly one should not say a blessing, at least not immediately, if it pulls one away from the mountain or flower or rainbow that one is engaging. And as we shall see in the next chapter, composing a blessing of one's own is an excellent response to moments of awe in wilderness. But I find the traditional blessings contribute to my spiritual practice for several reasons.

First, "reaction" blessings work because they give us words when we are speechless. Awesome events draw us closer and often we want to respond, to express our wonder at the mystery we are experiencing. Blessings enable us to do so when we have no words of our own.

For me, the best example of this dynamic is the short blessing one recites upon hearing of someone's death: *Baruch Dayan Emet*, "Blessed be the Truthful Judge." It has taken me years, but now I habitually respond to the news of someone's passing with these words. I find it enormously helpful.

When someone dies, the news is shocking and hurtful and ultimately mysterious. I am filled with emotion. I have no words. But in my befuddlement, I feel the need to respond. Keeping the intense emotion locked up is unsettling and painful. Saying the blessing releases the sad weight in my heart. I am saved the embarrassment of speaking words that I will immediately regret as insufficient in the face of death. And I am comforted. The blessing puts the horrible news into the big picture: all living things in this good world will inevitably die; without death there would be no life. Lastly, in saying a blessing, I share it all with God.

So too, nature blessings allow me to express my emotions when I am moved by the beauty and mystery of the natural world. I speak powerfully and appropriately at a time when composing my own words would distract me from the natural world and leave me feeling inadequate.

Second, the traditional blessings often draw us into an I-Thou encounter. Through the blessing, I focus outward in the present moment, forget about my own concerns, and enter receptive mode. Since the traditional blessings are short and I know them by heart, I don't get caught up in the words when I speak them. They serve more as a mantra than a thought.

When I set out in wilderness, I expect to feel awe. And I do. It's predictable in a place like the Grand Canyon. I am rarely surprised and startled. On the contrary, the more likely danger is that I will miss what is right in front of my eyes. By the third day on the trail, I take the landscape for granted. This is where a blessing changes everything. When I see a mountain or the ocean and habitually respond with the traditional blessing, it no longer needs to be business as usual. I can mumble the words by rote, of course, or I can listen to them. Then, the blessing shifts my awareness. A miracle is right before my eyes—if I am able and willing to see it properly.

Third, when a tradition is vital, it gives its adherents more than they could have invented themselves. It literally opens their eyes and enables them to experience the world in ways not possible without the insight and wisdom of previous generations. Notice that there are different blessings over different kinds of fragrances: the smell of blossoms on trees rather than shrubs, flowers as opposed to fruit. By learning the traditional blessings, I learn to see, smell, and appreciate the nuance and diversity of the natural world.

Finally, the blessing connects us to a larger meaning, namely, to Jewish ethics and Jewish history. This is best exemplified by the blessing over the rainbow. For those unfamiliar with the Book of Genesis, the rainbow blessing makes little sense. Why think of the covenant when seeing a natural wonder? But those familiar with this passage in the Torah know what the blessing connotes. After the Flood, God establishes a covenant with the creatures and humankind, promising to never again destroy life on earth. And then God says, "This is the sign that I set for the covenant between

Me and you, and every living creature with you, for all ages to come. I have set My bow in the clouds, and it shall serve as a sign of the covenant between Me and the earth" (Gen. 9:12–13).

Reciting the blessing not only expresses the awe, appreciation, and gratitude that I feel upon seeing a rainbow. It is also an opportunity to remember that all life is precious to God. I am reminded of the covenant, the relationship that grounds Jewish ethics and guides Jewish history. It's so much more than, "Whoa, dude, a rainbow!"

All the blessings are more than the sum of their particular words. Each one connects us to God, and God is the source of sanctity we might encounter in every facet of our lives—if only we could see what our eyes behold.

9

FILLING THE WORLD
WITH HOLINESS:
THE WAY OF BLESSING
PART II

> Everything created has a need to be hallowed and is capable of receiving it: all created corporeality, all created urges and elemental forces of the body. Hallowing enables the body to fulfill the meaning for which it was created.... Here, then, the world is neither transfigured into something wholly spiritual nor overcome by the spirit. The spirit does not embrace a holy world, rejoicing in its holiness, nor does it float above an unholy world, clutching all holiness to itself: it produces holiness, and the world is made holy.
>
> Martin Buber[1]

In our discussion of *kedushah,* "holiness," we have focused on *recognizing* the sacred in the natural world. But there is another aspect of holiness. As human beings, we are privileged to not only perceive *kedushah.* We help to *create* it.

FROM POTENTIAL TO ACTUAL

Endowed with discerning eyes, we humans can see the potential for goodness in any situation. And as creatures who enjoy self-consciousness, we know that in any given moment, we have a choice. We often act out of habit, but we know that with reflection and effort, we can choose to behave well. We can respond to tragedy with hope rather than despair; we can help a person in need rather than pass them by; we can act out of love rather than fear.

Everything and every being on earth, every thought and action, has the potential for *kedushah*, for holiness. But the key word is potential. So often, holiness does not manifest. When we lie, cheat, or, God-forbid, murder—when we act from *mochin d'katnut*, from small-mindedness—the potential lies untapped and dormant.

Holiness, then, must be actualized. The potential becomes real in the world through right perception, thought, and action. This is one of the great virtues of being a human being. We not only recognize *kedushah*, we spread it!

Traditional theology sees this as a spiritual process. In fulfilling the ritual and ethical commandments, we increase our awareness of *kedushah*. Holiness increases in the world because it fills up more of human consciousness. Strengthening awareness of the holy is more than enough justification for adopting spiritual practice.

As a mystic, I have a somewhat different perspective. I believe that the spiritual and physical aspects of reality can never be truly separated. They are different in degree, not in essence. The "physical" is denser than the "spiritual," but both are part of the *shefa*, the River of Light, the flow of divine energy that animates the world. *Chiut* is the tangible presence of God in the world. And as mentioned previously,[2] I believe in the radical assertion of the Kabbalah that just as God affects us, we affect God. The River runs both ways. Here's how I think it works.

All is potentially holy because the world is made of god-stuff and the *shefa* is constantly flowing through it. Our thoughts and actions channel the *chiut*. We block, divert, or quicken the flow of divine energy in the world. When we live in receptive mode and enter I-Thou, we direct the *shefa* into the here and now of our lives. We increase the *chiut* flowing through us and through our Thou. We draw the right balance of divine energy, of compassion and justice, into our spot in the universe.

So when we act rightly, *kedushah* increases not only in human heads, but in the universe as a whole. This is why those who have developed their sensitivities can *feel* the sacred in Torah scrolls and under wedding canopies, in sanctuaries and on mountaintops, where prayers have been offered over time. When I sense the *kedushah* in a chapel or a meditation hall, I'm not projecting, I'm responding.

The process doesn't affect only me. Other people might well perceive the holiness I helped create. Certainly, others enjoy the ethical responsibility I acquire in I-Thou. Spiritual practice is for the benefit of all creation.

Whether your theology is traditional or mystical, blessings are a key part of Judaism's strategy to spread holiness throughout the world. Blessings change our awareness. They nudge us into receptive mode and prepare us for I-Thou relation. When they succeed, the world becomes, not holier than thou, but holier through the Thou.

Prayer and ritual, when done with sincerity and heart, put us into conversation with the world: the dialogue of perceiving, engaging, and spreading holiness.

PRACTICES

COMPOSE YOUR OWN PERSONAL BLESSINGS

Once upon a time, before the invention of the printing press and even before the creation of the Jewish prayer service, Jews did not learn blessings from teachers or books. In fact, the traditional blessings were not invented by rabbis sitting around a table in the study hall. Rather, they were composed by people going about their lives.

The morning prayer service, usually prayed in synagogue, begins with a series of one-line blessings. Here are seven of them. The *Baruch atah* formula is followed by specific things for which we are grateful. Blessed be You, God, for

1. giving the rooster understanding to differentiate between day and night
2. making me in the divine image
3. making me free
4. making me a Jew
5. giving sight to the blind
6. dressing the naked
7. making firm our steps

Blessings 2, 3, and 4 are what I call theological blessings. They thank God for large, general gifts: freedom, the godliness inherent in human beings, Jewish identity. It's tempting to interpret the last three in similar fashion. But in fact, blessings 4, 5, and 6 address the concrete situation of the person's life. I call them practical blessings. The tip-off is the very first blessing. In it, we thank God "for giving the rooster understanding to differentiate between day and night." As we saw above, for us this would be the equivalent of blessing our alarm clocks. Reform prayer books understandably reinterpret it *sans* rooster (thanking God for giving us mind and instinct), as Jews today rarely have roosters. Conservative and Orthodox Jews recite it verbatim out of loyalty to the tradition. Once a prayer makes it into the prayer book, it is not to be removed. All of them miss the point. The morning blessings are not about theological principles or loyalty to the tradition. Rather, they are about seeing God in our daily lives.

For most of human history, the cry of the rooster was the first thing a person heard in the morning. While still in bed, pious Jews would recite the first blessing of the day. Then they would open their eyes, the occasion for thanking God for sight (blessing 5). Then they would get dressed, expressing gratitude for the very fact that we have clothes (blessing 6). Then they would bless God for the ability to walk (blessing 7). When you look at these blessings in a prayer book, you notice that the last one thanks God for removing the sleep from our eyes. The morning blessings were originally meant to be prayed first thing in the morning, as one gets out of bed.

Alas, Judaism as a religious practice is entering its fourth millennium. What were once spontaneous blessings that ordinary Jews recited without rabbis and prayer books have been codified, reified, canonized, and printed. These blessings have been divorced from their original context. What was once the profound practice of starting the day in the attitude of gratitude has turned into a list of theological principles disconnected from the actual experiences of one's life.

But composing one's own blessings in response to life's encounters is a venerable Jewish practice. We can recover it. In fact, the tradition encourages us: a pious Jew is instructed to say a hundred blessings a day! What better place than wilderness?

In the previous chapter, we learned the traditional blessings that might be said in response to the awe we feel in wilderness. In this practice, we offer our own spontaneous, creative blessings in the natural world.

Practice 19
PERSONAL BLESSINGS

1. Dedicate a time, while you are in your Soul-O spot or walking down the trail, to compose your own personal blessings. You might start with the traditional blessing formula:

> *Baruch atah Adonai Eloheinu Melech ha'olam* …
> Praised be You Adonai, our God, Sovereign of the universe …

2. Others are more comfortable with an alternative formula that includes feminine language and different images for God, such as the following:

> *B'ruchah at Yah, Ruach ha'olam* …
> Blessed be You, Spirit of the universe …

or

> *B'ruchah at Yah, Shechinat ha'olam* …
> Blessed be You, the *Shechinah* [God's immanent presence] of the universe …

3. Continue in English, or if you can, in Hebrew, and compose your blessing, for example:

> *Baruch atah Adonai Eloheinu Melech ha'olam*, for the cool wind on my sweaty face.
> *B'ruchah at Yah, Ruach ha'olam*, for the deep shades of green in the shiny leaves of this oak tree and the hum of the hummingbird.

There is no such thing as a wrong blessing. Personally I prefer to use at least some language from the tradition, but you might choose a different introduction if other words better enable you to make the blessing meaningful. (Be sure you are blessing God and not the tree or the waterfall alone. Otherwise, we run into problems with idolatry. See appendix 2.)

My only rule: relate your blessing to what you are actually seeing, touching, hearing, feeling. Try to avoid generalities, such as blessing God for the animals, the generic color green (contrast to the example above), or the ability to hear. As much as possible, the goal is to integrate into the specific situation. The more detail, the better. Blessings should be said out loud, but a whisper will do.

ALTERNATE PERSONAL AND TRADITIONAL BLESSINGS IN A "BLESSINGS WALK"

Partly out of respect for Jewish tradition, partly because the wisdom of previous generations sets an example and opens our eyes to experience we are not likely to attain on our own, I like to balance my personal blessings with traditional ones.

BLESSINGS WALK

1. To begin the morning prayer service, take a "blessings walk."

2. Alternate the traditional morning blessings, found at the beginning of the *Shacharit* morning service, with spontaneous blessings over what you are seeing, touching, and hearing in the moment.

For example, after reciting the traditional Hebrew morning blessing,

> Praised be You Adonai, our God, Sovereign of the universe, who enables the blind to see,

you might follow with,

> Praised be You, the Source of blessing, who in Her wisdom sends gray mist to cover the granite walls of this canyon.

One might continue with the next traditional blessing, this time phrased in the feminine,

> Praised be You, the *Shechinah* filling the universe, who dresses the naked,

followed by,

> Praised be You, the Spirit of the universe, who gives me high-tech layers and a waterproof jacket to keep me warm.

HEART-SONG IN
THE HEART-LAND:
JEWISH PRAYER IN WILDERNESS

> Every evening we recite: "He creates light and
> makes the dark." Twice a day we say: "He is one."
> What is the meaning of such repetition? A scientific
> theory, once it is announced and accepted, does not
> have to be repeated twice a day. The insights of
> wonder must be constantly kept alive. Since there is
> a need for daily wonder, there is a need for daily
> worship.
>
> Abraham Joshua Heschel[1]

For me, praying the traditional Jewish prayers in wilderness can so
enliven them that sometimes the words seem to jump off the
page. Just speaking to God in God's handiwork is exhilarating.
But relating to the siddur, the Jewish prayer book, is enormously
difficult for most Jews today. We rarely acknowledge just how
daunting it is.

It's difficult because meaningful prayer is emotional, intuitive,
and creative, right-brain functions, but reading words from a book
activates the left side of the brain. It's difficult because it is a greater
challenge to put your heart into someone else's words than into
your own. It's difficult because we might not agree with what a

given prayer is saying. It's difficult because the traditional prayers are in Hebrew.

But I believe that it is worth the effort to meet these challenges.

THE POWER OF TRADITION: WISDOM AND GROUNDING

For starters, praying words that have been uttered in prayer for thousands of years by millions of people is grounding. I am sometimes moved to tears by it. Even when one is alone in wilderness, the siddur is a direct link to the tradition and the community. In this alienating world, we are at home anywhere we open a siddur.

Traditions are not only repositories of wisdom, they make wisdom possible. Traditions give us the vocabulary and concepts, the beliefs and norms, to express ourselves. After all, without that verbal product of community, language, we wouldn't even be able to speak to ourselves, let alone to others. When a tradition is vibrant, it opens up our eyes to knowledge and experience we would not have found on our own.

And just as important, traditions ground our creativity. There is no such thing as a great writer who isn't a great reader. As part of their training, jazz students learn the improvisations of their great predecessors note for note from sheet music. Successful artists do not ignore the techniques, styles, and accomplishments of their artistic tradition. Rather, they master them. Then they can improvise in ways that bring their art to a new level.

Prayer, too, is an art. What matters is whether one's prayer is heartfelt, sincere, passionate, honest, insightful—truly open to God. But there are rules, forms, and structures, which, if mastered, raise the level of our artistry in prayer. To even know what prayer is requires that we learn from a prayer tradition.

The traditional prayers in the siddur do not always express what I need to say to God in any given moment. But often they do. And even when they do not, they model for me the great artistry of prayer.

Lastly, traditional Jewish prayer nurtures humility.

HUMILITY AND SURRENDER

Humility is a key ingredient in spiritual practice. It is the all-important move one makes to get beyond egoism and selfishness by listening. In I-Thou, we surrender to the needs of the Thou. In tapping into the wisdom of a tradition, we humbly submit to the masters of the past. This is often done quite literally. Whether music, art, sports, or graduate studies, we apprentice ourselves to the great teachers of the generation, not to become underlings, but to foster our own creativity.

In spiritual practice, a tradition serves as the trusted vehicle to which one may humbly, and safely, surrender to God. Wherever I have gone, whether among Jewish, Christian, Native American, Daoist, or Buddhist teachers, they are critical of New Age spirituality on this point. Those who pick and choose among the various practices of different traditions face a danger. Because they have not journeyed deeply into, that is, surrendered to, any one tradition, they may lack spiritual depth themselves. There is, of course, much to gain in tailoring rituals and prayers to one's personal situation. But if it is not balanced by a tradition's wisdom and discipline, a narcissistic spirituality can result. The problem with "create your own myth" and "make your own ceremony" spirituality is its inability to foster self-transcendence. It is extremely difficult to surrender to a ritual of one's own creation. I myself constantly struggle with this, for the benefits of ritual creativity are also clear. The best solution I know is to consciously seek a balance by placing one's creativity within a trusted tradition.

For all the above reasons, it is worthwhile to learn traditional Jewish prayer. Learning Hebrew is difficult, but it is not as hard as you might think.[2]

A PERSONAL RELATIONSHIP
WITH IMPERSONAL GOD

Prayer is a major vehicle for reaching out to God. It helps to know that God might respond. This is somewhat easier for those who maintain a traditional theology in which God is experienced as a person who talks to us more or less the way we talk to God.

It is more difficult for the mystics among us, who recognize God as the *shefa*, the divine flow, a force in an open-ended universe for which there is no master plan. How can a force be intelligent? Can we pray to a flow? Does it do any good if God does not control the future?

First things first. While I myself don't see God as all-powerful and all-controlling, I do not see God as nonexistent or withdrawn from the world, either. As you know, I think God affects us profoundly. I-Thou moments attract us with beauty, draw us to love, and command us ethically. In such moments we discover the profound meaning of our lives. The either/or that fundamentalists sometimes try to foist on the rest of us, all-powerful God or no God, is a false choice.

But if God is more than a person, and if I don't perceive God as a personality, to whom might I pray? How might there be a response?

Can I establish a personal relationship with impersonal God?

GOD-TALK: THE ART OF METAPHOR

As religious thinkers have noted over the millennia, using words at all to talk about that which is beyond words, to describe God, is problematic. But there is little choice. While silence in this area is often admirable, we need to articulate and share our experiences of divinity. Meaning needs to be communicated, both to others and to ourselves. So we turn to the language of poetry, to metaphor. We image God as a parent, a king, a friend, a healer, or a teacher not because God actually is one of those human identities. Rather, our relation to God is partially analogous to the ways we connect to our parents, doctors, and teachers. Metaphor is also the way we personalize, and make understandable, abstract ideas or nonpersonal realities. Some conceive of the homeland as a father. Ships are likened by their (mostly male) sailors to women. We might give our car a name.

My favorite example is from Jewish life. Shabbat is a day, a measurement in time. A certain number of hours is about as abstract as you can get. But if you have observed Shabbat over time, you know that Shabbat has a different "feel" than any other day. Never mind the perfectly reasonable explanation (you don't work, you go to synagogue, you have gourmet meals with family and friends) that accounts for the felt, bodily experience of Shabbat. The fact is people develop an irrational, emotional attachment to this unit of time. Shabbat is something we encounter. It has a personality. And to speak of this, it makes perfect sense (pun intended) to call Shabbat, in the words of the kabbalists, a bride or a queen. We personally interact with the sacred character, the holiness, of the day.[3]

Which metaphors shall I use for God, this more-than-a-person (indeed, more-than-anything-I-know) reality, which I perceive as a force possessing intelligence and will?

As discussed earlier, the kabbalist's metaphor for the *shefa*, the River of Light, best models my experience of God. A river is always rushing toward me. Divinity is always coming my way. And how I stand in it influences the flow. So my experience of the river has a lot to do with my own willpower, decisions, and actions. I can swim upstream or float along.

What I can't control is the flow and course of the river. Sometimes the waters are still and I'm so busy watching television or cooking a meal, I can forget that I'm in it at all. At other times I go over a waterfall and I can't help but be aware of the river.[4]

But the key point is that I experience a river personally. When I paddle this way or that, the river pushes me in response. It may send me along my course or divert me to a new direction I did not intend. But the river's response to my action is unique to me. It pushes me in this direction at this time, and no one else.

So, too, do I understand my relation to the River of Light. Because of my inability to live in receptive mode, often I am hardly aware of it. But when I enter I-Thou, the river "speaks" to me loud and clear. I have no idea what it will say. Sometimes it demands justice and makes me uncomfortable, sometimes I feel overwhelming love. Sometimes I am humbled and contrite, other times empowered and energized. The encounter with God is spontaneous and open-ended. Most important, it is always profound and meaningful in a personal way. God has "spoken" to me about my life in this moment in this place.

I live in personal relationship with impersonal God.

The kabbalists capture this when they say that the ten aspects or spheres of divinity comprise what scholars call the "godhead," the totality of God's knowable self in the cosmos. It is as impersonal a name for God as it gets. Each sphere represents different aspects of the divine—mercy, judgment, beauty, love, strength, and the like. Depending on what people think, say, and do, people interact with the sphere that their behavior has merited. From the impersonal godhead they have received a personalized rejoinder (see chapter 4).

Prayer makes us conscious of the fact that we are always standing in the *shefa*. It moves me along the spiritual path, toward receptive mode. And when I say You to the sacred One—standing with senses open, fully aware of this precious world—I am likely to feel the press of holiness against me, a window of I-Thou in an I-It world. I receive a response to my thoughts, words, feelings, and fears in this moment of my life. God has answered my prayer.

ON TRADITIONAL PRAYERS
AND RITUALS

P'SUKEI D'ZIMRAH: THE POETICS OF PRAISE

If there is a word I dislike in the religious vocabulary of English-speaking liberal Judaism, it is "worship." In any other context, the word has negative connotations. Worship is usually associated with the attitude of an immature person toward the idol of their affection. In religious context, it fits hierarchal, patriarchal images of God.

The liturgy typically associated with worship is the psalms, as they lavish God with ever-higher crescendos of praise. So for many years, I did not like the psalms. I was leery of the incessant praise for God we find in the Jewish prayer book. If God is so great and we are so lowly, does God really need our approval?

I still don't like the word "worship," but as my spiritual life progressed, I came to appreciate the wisdom of the Jewish tradition in packing the opening section of the morning service, the *P'sukei d'Zimrah* (verses of praise), with psalms and other prayers of praise. Like gratitude (see chapter 7), offering praise changes our mind-state and opens our eyes to holiness in the world. It's amazing how people respond positively to those who are quick to praise others. We so enjoy being around individuals who communicate their excitement for us instead of critical types who build themselves up by putting others down.

The specific function of praise is that it moves us into a place of humility. This is the essential ingredient of entering receptive mode, of being an I that can encounter a Thou. Praise differs from gratitude in that it simply extols the virtues of the other. It does not report on what the other has done for me or my own thankfulness. Rather, words of praise communicate our deep appreciation. When we wish to put wonder and awe into language, when it is time to express the admiration and love in our hearts, we turn to the poetics of praise.

For more on psalms, see practice 15.

YOTZER OR AND MA'ARIV ARAVIM: GOD IN THE NATURAL WORLD

One of the great obstacles between us and the traditional prayers is the difficulty of putting our own feelings and emotions into the words of others. This is compounded by the cultural walls around the prayers: they are written in Hebrew; they reflect a mind-set two thousand years removed from ours; we may not agree with the theology they express. What's a Jew to do?

For starters, it is worth noting that the human condition is different, but not so different from that of our ancestors. We can relate to much of their concerns and hopes, especially if we place ourselves in their shoes by imagining ourselves in the context of ancient times. Often this is difficult, but not when the liturgy turns to nature. The sun rises and sets for us just as it did for them.

The *Yotzer Or* and *Ma'ariv Aravim*, located directly after the *Bar'chu*, the Call to Worship, and before the *Sh'ma* in the morning and evening services, respectively, are quintessential nature prayers. Before going on to the specifics of God's relationship with the Jewish people, we recognize God's connection to the earth. To understand the intent of the writers, to make these words our own, we don't need to research their origins in the library. We simply need to see a sunset or explore a wilderness. Clearly, the liturgists of old felt wonder and awe in the natural world just like us.

Notice that in the *Yotzer Or*, God's creation of the cosmos, an event in the past, is phrased in the present tense. My favorite line in the entire liturgy just might be the following, from *Yotzer Or*: *uv'tuvo m'chadeish b'chol yom tamid ma'asei v'reisheet*, "in goodness, God renews every day, always, the works of creation."

As *v'reisheet* (or *b'reisheet*) actually means "in the beginning," it comes to connote "creation" because of the word before it: *ma'a-sei* (works). This nonliteral meaning of *b'reisheet* has become part of modern Israeli Hebrew. As Hebrew went unspoken for hundreds of years, Israelis needed to invent quite a number of new words in revitalizing the language for our times. One such word was "wilderness." They chose a phrase based on this prayer: *eretz b'reisheet* (land of creation).[5]

We, of course, know what the authors of this prayer did not. As evolution proceeds, as species evolve, continents move, and mountain ranges rise, the creation of the world indeed continues. Yet they too knew that God's involvement with the world is not a static, one-time event in the past. Jewish mysticism developed from verses like this. The mystics understood "renewing creation" as evidence of the *shefa*, the River of Light, continually bringing divine life-force into the world.

TALLIT (PRAYER SHAWL) AND *TEFILLIN* (PHYLACTERIES): INVOLVE THE BODY

My vision quest teacher, John Milton, taught his students that every day one should state his or her intention to reach enlightenment. Until that moment, I never truly understood the importance of the first major commandment Jews are asked to perform every weekday: to wrap ourselves in *tallit* and *tefillin*.[6] It is the daily Jewish intention ceremony. We cannot start the day without taking note of the big picture and what's really important in life.

I particularly love these practices because they involve the body. Especially in wilderness, when my senses are alive and kicking, the touch of *tallit* and *tefillin* against the skin is particularly invigorating. I am tangibly reminded that the source of prayer is not the disembodied mind, but the heart's response to a sensuous body's engagement with the world.

PRACTICES

TAKE YOUR TIME

I have prayed in synagogues the world over. I can testify. Many adjectives and adverbs might be applied to traditional Jewish prayer. "Slowly" is not among them.

I have also been to many spiritual retreats. I remember with particular fondness the weeklong retreats during the first Mindfulness Leadership Training program at Elat Chayyim. What was so profound? Every day we were given an hour to daven, to pray, the morning service in silence. Even though I was a rabbi with long experience in Jewish prayer, I had never prayed the entire service, slowly, day after day. The siddur has never been the same to me since.

I discovered the deep artistry of the prayers, the great lyricism and poetry of the liturgists, as I listened to words I spoke in a whisper. I had time to let their meanings sink in. Some upset me, others thrilled me. Since I had nowhere else to go, my concentration was spared the distractions of my usually frenetic mind. And I had time to put awareness squarely on my heart. Yearning flowed into the words of the prayers.

Practice 21
PRAY SLOWLY

1. Allow yourself enough time to pray from the traditional prayer book, the siddur, at your leisure. If you do not have time to pray the entire service slowly, then choose one or two prayers for your special, slow attention.

2. Speak the words slowly in a whisper.

3. Alternatively, try *davenen* (praying) the prayers Hasidic style. Say or sing the words out loud in simple, improvised melodic

phrases of your choosing (somewhere between Jewish hip-hop and a chant mantra). This works just as well in English as in Hebrew.

Praying slowly goes a long way toward overcoming the obstacle of putting one's own heart into someone else's words.

MEMORIZE YOUR FAVORITE PRAYERS

Many pious Jews know the prayers by heart, which unfortunately helps them to pray in fifth gear. But memorization can also allow us to slow down and fully engage the words. Visually undistracted, attention can be placed on their sound and cadence. We can concentrate fully on the meaning of the words. Alternatively, we can use the prayers like a mantra. Free of the right-brain act of reading, we can allow the sounds of the words to quiet our minds and ease us into receptive mode.

It is in wilderness, however, that the full benefits of memorization are realized. When standing in one of God's awesome cathedrals, *one need not choose between praying the prayer or looking up.* In this practice, *the Torah/nature divide is fully overcome!*

Praying psalms or prayers that speak of the natural world, in the natural world, heightens my sensual experience. Memorization helps us connect to the liturgy and wild nature at the same time. Concepts and perceptions, past and present, body and spirit—they are all present, all at once, in the act of prayer in wilderness.

Practice 22
MEMORIZE A PRAYER

1. Choose a prayer or psalm, and commit it to memory.

2. Pray with your eyes open in wilderness.

3. Try leaving part of your awareness on your body, as in meditative walking (see practice 2).

4. If you are blessed with an insight, you might write about it in your journal.

FIND YOUR *PASUK* (VERSE)

When Rabbi Shefa Gold[7] studies a psalm or traditional prayer, she looks for the verse that best summarizes its theme or message. This is the power *pasuk*, which for her then becomes the lyrics for a chant.

Practice 23
CARRY A POWER *PASUK*

1. While (slowly!) praying or studying a psalm or traditional prayer from a place of mindfulness, listen for your power *pasuk*, the verse that speaks loud and clear to you.

2. Memorize the verse and carry it with you the rest of the day. Repeat it as you hike. Make it a mantra while cooking dinner or gazing at a lake. See what it has to teach you.

3. If you were blessed with an insight, you might write about it in your journal.

4. Write the verse down in a special section of your journal, where you can add other verses later.

SUNRISE, SUNSET

Rabbi Arthur Green is one of the world's leading scholars of Jewish mystical thought. Together with Rabbi Lawrence Kushner, he is the voice of contemporary Jewish mysticism in liberal Jewry. In his book, *Ehyeh: A Kabbalah for Tomorrow* (Jewish Lights), he makes a simple but profound suggestion.[8]

Practice 24
PRAY AT SUNRISE OR SUNSET

1. Find a place to pray, preferably with a view, just before sunrise or sunset.

2. As you will be in the darkness, bring a headlamp or flashlight.

3. Be sure to listen before speaking; the sounds of wildlife increase at dawn and dusk.

These special times, when light and dark intermingle, remind us of beginnings and endings, of birth and death. And they are extraordinarily beautiful. Wonder and awe are likely in the neighborhood. These are the natural times to pray in the natural world.

THE ART OF PERSONAL PRAYER

I was a rabbi, and well into my forties, before I took personal prayer seriously. I never did it much, if at all, until I found myself at ... a Buddhist meditation retreat.

For whatever reason, and I'm not sure this is a good thing, I don't have much fear of jumping into a pool to see if I can swim. After my first experience with a four-day, partially silent retreat, I asked my teacher, Sylvia Boorstein, if she would recommend a longer sit. A few months later, I began a six-week residential, fully silent retreat. What was I thinking! Three days in, I began to pray like there was no tomorrow. "Please God, get me out of here!"

But I stuck it out. And I found my prayer voice.

We all have one. In Jewish circles like mine, however, it was never encouraged. Then, as today, Jewish educators were so caught up in teaching the traditional prayers, (correctly) concerned that the ethnic identity of young Jews is connected to the traditional prayer book, they didn't see much value in teaching personal prayer. But this, of course, is backwards. Praying someone else's words to God is much harder than praying your own, and if you don't have a spiritual rationale for personal prayer, you won't likely have one for communal prayer either.

The obstacles to personal prayer begin with a lack of belief in its efficacy. I have shared my own experience above. There are many other approaches. (See Resources for suggested reading.) Every spiritual seeker must find their own way in this regard. Another obstacle is the simple fact that we have to take the time and make the effort to do it. But that's not difficult to overcome. Rather, the biggest obstacle is that most Western Jews are just not used to doing it. It's not part of our culture.

This is a local phenomenon. In fact, personal prayer has been part of Jewish culture in other places, past and present. The prayer book is a very late addition to Jewish life.[9] While some fixed prayers, like the *Sh'ma*, go back thousands of years, communal prayer leaders were *expected* to improvise their own prayers well into the Middle Ages. As part of their revival of Jewish spirituality in modern times, the Hasidim emphasized personal prayer.

Fortunately, personal prayer itself is not difficult. Start a sentence, "Please God ..." or "May it be ..." and the rest follows.

Another way to begin is to pray for another person, particularly someone who is ill. Like the proverbial soldier in the foxhole, nothing gets one over the supposed irrationality of prayer than expressing your wishes for a loved one's health. Indeed, the traditional *Mi Shebeirach* prayer for the sick, which I never heard growing up in Reform circles, is now a prominent part of the liturgy. (You'll find it after the Torah blessings in the Shabbat morning service.)

Reciting the *Mi Sheberiach* is an excellent way to start your personal prayer practice. Alternatively, just begin a sentence, "May it be your will, God, that so and so …" or "Please God, may you (the person who is ill) be…" and follow with your wishes of health, wisdom, protection from harm, and so on, for another person.

I have since realized why personal, spontaneous prayer came so easily during that six-week silent retreat. For one thing, I had plenty of time. (The traditional prayers also came alive, because I didn't rush through them.) But more significant, I prayed from a place of mindfulness. Like every retreatant, I spent day and night observing my thoughts and emotions and their bodily interactions with the world. I learned an incredible amount about myself.

This is probably a guy thing, but I was socialized to be strong in the world. I never thought about the reasons for my weaknesses. I only thought about how to get around them. But as spiritual life has ripened, I have come to understand that the greatest warrior is the one who takes on his or her inner fears, something much harder than the fear of walking over a river on a wet log or camping alone. Now I try to accept my vulnerability rather than deny it. And I have learned the Buddhist lesson: everything changes, you can't stop it or control it. You can only learn to live with it. So I have come to understand the limits of my personal strength. I need the help of others. And I need that mysterious quality that I am lost without: *chesed*, divine grace and loving-kindness.

In short, mindfulness helps me to understand myself and the world with increasing clarity. And that has changed my prayer life. Here is what I have discovered.

When you know what you truly need, spontaneous prayer arises on its own.

After a while, prayer becomes effortless, as easy and natural as breathing.

Practice 25
PERSONAL PRAYER

1. When possible, use any of the mindfulness practices in *A Wild Faith* to get still and enter receptive mode. (Sometimes, you know what you need without practicing a specific mindfulness exercise, but in general, it's helpful.)

2. Compose your own prayer to God. The simplest way is to begin a sentence with "Please God ..." or "May it be ..." or "May I receive your help/wisdom/care ..." or in praying for others, "Please God, may you be ...," and let the rest follow.

3. Be as honest as possible. What do you really need? (It isn't a Jaguar.) What do others really need? What are your best hopes for the world, for yourself? In prayer, simplicity is a virtue. The idea is to say words that, as much as possible, come directly from your emotional center. When prayer is heartfelt, it carries an emotional charge.

4. You might end with a traditional blessing, such as:

בָּרוּךְ אַתָּה יהוה שׁוֹמֵעַ תְּפִלָּה.

Baruch atah Adonai shomei'a tefilah.
Praised be You, Adonai, who hears prayer.

Spontaneous, personal prayer is an appropriate end to nearly every practice in *A Wild Faith*. Just as spiritual practice benefits from the setting of intentions, it also benefits from the emotional discharge and formal letting go—the closure—a blessing can provide.

11

WITH YOUR WHOLE SELF:
LIVING IN YOUR BODY

> Man stands created, a whole body, ensouled by his
> relation to the created, enspirited by his relation to
> the Creator. It is to the whole man, in this unity of
> body, soul, and spirit, that the Lord of Revelation
> comes ... it is not only with his thought and his feel-
> ings, but with the sole of his foot and the tip of his
> finger as well....
>
> **Martin Buber**[1]

The first blessing in the Jewish prayer service after the *Sh'ma*, the
V'ahavta, is central in the consciousness of the Jewish people. A
direct quote from the Torah, it reads, "You shall love Adonai your
God with all your heart and with all your soul [*nefesh*] and with all
your might" (Deut. 6:5).

Though usually rendered "soul," the word *nefesh* is best translated as "person," the way we might say, "Oh, that poor soul
deserved better." Unlike the postbiblical notion of a soul, the
nefesh of the Torah, whether human or animal, eats food. Scholar
Joel Hoffman concludes that what is usually translated as "heart"
and "soul" in our prayer (*b'chol l'vav'cha u'v'chol nafsh'cha*) was in
fact a biblical idiom for "the whole person."[2] Since *nefesh* also refers

117

to the animals, the word clearly includes what we have in common with them: our bodies.

The command to love God applies not only to intellect and emotions, but to the body as well!

THE LIVING LAND AND
THE SENSING BODY

It's amazing when you think about it. The bizarre sound of a frog croaking can nevertheless evoke wonder and joy. Wherever we go in the natural world, enchantment awaits. Our emotions seem wired to our sensual involvement with sunsets, streams, and flowers. The spaciousness of a wide-open desert horizon creates spaciousness in the heart, while a fog-filled Sierra canyon with softened colors and limited visibility induces feelings of intimacy and vulnerability.

This is hardly surprising. It is our bodily senses that perceive the natural world, and our senses are most alive in the place where they evolved: the wilderness. In the city, our senses often feel under assault. We actually try to turn them off at times to avoid advertisements or block out the grating noise of trucks and lawn mowers. Much of the time, our senses are underutilized as we navigate the predictable urban terrain and stare at two-dimensional pages and TV screens.

In the natural world, everything we perceive is in motion. Even the mountains are moving, if on a schedule of their own. Plants and animals, the weather and the elements, they are always stirring, always improvising. Particularly with animals, we don't know where they are headed next. But we better bring all our senses to bear on the bear, lest we be caught unawares when she moves toward us![3]

When I am awestruck in wilderness, engaged in moments of I-Thou with rivers or rainbows or moose, I can hardly move my mouth. At most, an "Oh wow" or "My God" comes out. Yet, the moment is profound. But if my thinking mind is paralyzed, what is receiving the Thou? What perceives the sacred in the natural world?

In moments of awe, the mind goes mute, but the body is fully engaged.

THE WISDOM OF THE BODY

No one would disagree, I hope, with the notion that our bodies contain wisdom independent of our thinking. The various systems of my body are constantly adjusting to changes in the environment without my thinking about it, just as my foot plants in such a way as to maintain my balance when the incline of the trail changes. I may work on my basketball shot consciously during practice, but during the game, it happens on its own or I will not score many baskets. When I do try to alter my shot during practice, it is not enough to think about it. Rather, I implant the proper motion in my body memory through repetition and practice.

Enlightenment ethical theory, in the wake of Western religious thought, saw the body as a source of temptation and evil. In order to act ethically, one needs to reason and then act without the interference of the bodily passions. It is only in the last generation or so that our culture has begun to move beyond this fallacy. The mind/body dualism that grounds such thinking is being disproved in many fields, including philosophy, psychology, and perhaps most significantly, medicine.

One of the tribulations that autistic people often face is a revulsion to touch. Many cannot stand to be embraced. Sometimes an autistic person is touched on one part of the body and feels it in another. Researchers note that these same people also have trouble making everyday, commonsense decisions. They struggle to tell the difference between a stranger who comes to genuinely befriend them or one who seeks their trust in order to steal from them. In other words, the people who according to mind/body dualism should think best—people who avoid sensuous contact with the world—are the very people who have trouble thinking straight.[4]

Our abstract reasoning abilities are not inhibited by our bodies. Rather, it is the sensuous touch of our bodies with the world that enables us to think at all.

THE PASSIONATE BODY

Enlightenment thought, however, was indeed correct in identifying the correlation between passion and the body. If you want to know whether a person is happy or depressed, telling the truth or telling a lie, are you going to give more credence to their words or their body "language"? As my Buddhist teachers like to say, "The mind has many ruses, but the body does not lie." The body is indeed home to our emotions.

Both thought and emotion, then, require bodies. And of course, so does our perception of the world. For me, it is simply inconceivable that we could know anything without our bodies. So if we want to put intuition, emotion, and body wisdom into our spiritual practice, if we want to express our passionate desire to connect with God, we are shooting ourselves in the foot if we fail to involve ourselves physically.

This is especially true for those of us who discern God as the *shefa*, the River of Light, as well as for those of us who meet God in I-Thou relation. We do not reason God or think God. Rather, we perceive God. Some say we humans have a sixth, spiritual sense beyond the physical senses that detects the divine.[5] It makes more *sense* to me that we perceive God like we perceive everything else—through our bodies.

PRACTICES

NOTICE HOW THE LANDSCAPES AFFECT YOU

Everyone knows that our physical surroundings have an impact on us. It matters if we have a cubicle or an office window, if the climate is mostly overcast or sunny, if the yard is green from plants and trees or gray from concrete. In the following exercise, we take this insight seriously.

NOTICE WHAT THE LANDSCAPE EVOKES IN YOUR HEART

1. While hiking, skiing, kayaking, or embarking in other outdoor activities, keep part of your awareness on your body, as in meditative walking (see practice 2).

2. As you focus on the natural world, notice the emotions that the landscape evokes in you. See if certain landscapes tend to elicit similar emotions over time.

3. If you can, return to the same spot at different times. Do different seasons, temperatures, or times of day elicit different feelings?

4. If you like, record your observations in your journal.

Some landscapes are lush, others barren; sometimes the water is salty and crashing with waves, other times clear and still; sometimes you enjoy wide horizons, other times an intimate canyon, surrounded by trees.

Sometimes the same view yields an entirely different landscape at different times: midday versus sunset; a flash flood versus a dry wash; storm clouds versus clear skies.

When we put our awareness on our bodies, we notice that different landscapes really *feel* different from each other—viscerally.

121

This is a deceptive exercise. It seems easy but in fact is quite subtle. First, we learn to differentiate between our projections and our perceptions. When we are emotionally charged, our feelings impact what we see. When the emotion is a reaction to the landscape, that's excellent. If we're angry about something that happened before we left home, not so good. To truly "feel" the landscape, we must calm our minds, enter receptive mode, and see with our senses. If we get emotional after that ... excellent!

Over time, you will notice that certain psychic states arise in certain landscapes. You might be calmer in some places than others. (For me, that would be a place near flowing water.) Other landscapes might induce a bit of anxiety (a dark, decaying forest). Most people's spirits soar on a mountain peak with a great view. Again, it takes refined discrimination to differentiate between what the landscape is evoking in you and what you bring to the encounter. Are your spirits high on the peak because you "conquered" the mountain or "mastered" a difficult route, or because the infinite view sensitizes you to Infinite Spirit?

CHANT

Music deeply affects us for a simple reason: we experience it bodily. If you have any doubts about this, place your hand over your chest cavity and sing. Feel your body resonate with the sound. Notice the difference when you sing AAAHHH or EEEEEE or OOOHHHMMM.

Chant is singing in a meditative mode, not so different from the Hasidic *nigun* or wordless song mentioned above. The melody should be simple. The woman who is revitalizing chant as a Jewish practice, Rabbi Shefa Gold, teaches that when we encounter a good chant, it's as if we already knew it. It also needs to be simple because it needs to be boring. No, you didn't read a misprint. It needs to be boring. As Rabbi Gold teaches, boredom precedes breakthrough. A chant works the same way as a mantra does in sitting meditation. When we bore our analytic thinking mind, it is lulled to sleep, allowing us to live in our bodies. In chanting, we sing simple words in a simple melody far too many times. Like any mindfulness practice that plants us in the present and directs awareness away from our egos, we are clearing heart-space and sculpting a heart-vessel for the *shefa* to fill.

When ending a chant, it is quite easy to let our minds wander and start thinking about lunch plans. But this, teaches Rabbi Gold, is a critical moment. Here is where we discover what the chant has changed in us. If we remain in receptive mode, we receive the world around us with fresh, calm attention.

Since I can't teach you chant in this book, let me recommend Rabbi Gold's CDs and the recordings on her website (www. rabbishefagold.com). I'd also suggest attending a retreat with her or another teacher of chant.

Practice 27
CHANT IN WILDERNESS

1. Choose a chant with words that might enhance your connection with wild nature.

2. In other settings, it is sometimes useful to chant with eyes shut. But in wilderness, we attempt to connect to the natural world around us. Chant with half of your awareness on your body, and half on what your eyes behold and your ears hear. If you do close your eyes to concentrate on your heart, keep awareness on your body and the natural world through your other senses (as in Vipassana meditation).

3. Sing the chant too many times. Boredom precedes breakthrough.

4. As you sense your body while chanting, you may feel "stuck" in a particular place. Keep your attention on the spot, and it will likely relax.[6]

5. When you end the chant, be especially mindful. Enter receptive mode by following the breath and placing the rest of your awareness on your body and your heart (see practices 2 and 11).
6. If you are unfamiliar with Jewish chant, try any simple Hebrew song that you know, such as *Hinei mah tov u'mah na'im, shevet achim gam yachad* or *Oseh shalom bimromav, hu ya'aseh shalom aleinu v'al kol yisrael, v'imru, amen.* Or chant the *Sh'ma* (*Sh'ma yisrael, Adonai eloheinu, Adonai echad*).

These are my favorite chants from Rabbi Gold:

מַה־גָּדְלוּ מַעֲשֶׂיךָ יְהוָה מְאֹד עָמְקוּ מַחְשְׁבֹתֶיךָ׃

Mah gadlu ma'asecha Yah, m'od amku machsh'votecha.
How great are Your works, O God, how deep are Your thoughts. (Psalm 92:6)

מַה־נּוֹרָא הַמָּקוֹם הַזֶּה

Mah nora hamakom hazeh.
How awesome is this place. (Gen. 28:17)

וְנָהָר יֹצֵא מֵעֵדֶן לְהַשְׁקוֹת אֶת־הַגָּן

V'nahar yotzei mei'Eden, l'hashkot et hagan.
A river comes forth from Eden to water the garden. (Gen. 2:10)

MAKE MUSIC

On my last solo wilderness retreat, a four-day fast, I brought a Native American flute. Easy to play (just six notes in one scale), it was perfect for a less-than-professional musician like myself. I quickly discovered why jazz players call a saxophone an axe. I wore the flute in my belt and took it everywhere. I had no idea that it could affect my retreat so thoroughly.

Every time I rested between practices and my mind began to wander, that is, about one hundred times a day, I played the flute. The music exiled thought and brought my awareness right back to my body. All told, I played for several hours a day. I played for the river and the moon, the bees and the butterflies. As I got better, I played as part of my practice. I wailed on the flute to express anger; played softly to offer a prayer. I composed songs: a melody for my insecurity, an ode to the local birds, a dirge for the circle of dead trees that became the practice center of my Soul-O site.

Practice 28
PLAY A MUSICAL INSTRUMENT

1. Choose a simple instrument that you can carry. Flutes, whistles, and recorders are naturals. Some bring travel guitars or other large instruments. Percussion instruments are excellent because their sound is primal, you won't judge yourself on the beauty of your melodies, and most anyone can play them. Also, you can sing or chant while drumming.

2. As you play, enter receptive mode. Place your attention on the beings around you, or if you are doing *teshuvah*, on your heart. You might dedicate your song to God.

3. Others in the vicinity may or may not appreciate your music. Be sure that you are not disturbing other people nearby.

4. As with chant, when you finish playing, make the effort to stay in receptive mode. Listen to the world around you; notice the state of your heart.

This practice succeeds to the extent that we make the musical instrument an instrument of dialogue. As much as possible, we keep our awareness on the natural world or on our heart. The artistic value of the song is not important. We aren't composing music to show off to friends back home. Nor is the music meant to entertain us now or others later. Rather, the purpose is to stay in receptive mode. It should express our emotions and connect us to the natural world.

Three days before turning in the manuscript for this book, I sat on a river bank in Grand Teton National Park. As I was well hidden, a deer walked right by me into the river, less than five feet away. She did not see me until she was halfway across. She started to run, but by then I had the flute out of my pack. I played for the deer. She stopped on the opposite bank to listen, about twenty yards away. Occasionally she grazed, but for the most part, she stared at me, her big ears perked, then flopping in the breeze, then perked again. When my fingers tired, I sang to her; the Hebrew chant seemed to soothe her. Twenty minutes later, she had had enough and continued on her way.

Wild animals love music. They are also fascinated by our words. On a different retreat, I was visited every night by a skunk. It never skunked me, perhaps because I sang and talked to it in hushed tones.

FEEL THE DIVINE LIFE-FORCE

As discussed above, one reason we feel different in diverse landscapes is that the various elements and species have different energies. As your body awareness grows through the various mindfulness practices, particularly meditation and fasting, you will begin to notice this. I'll never forget the first time I approached a large ocotillo cactus. How different from the juniper tree on the hill above.

Practice 29
SENSE THE *CHIUT* IN THE NATURAL WORLD

1. To purposely feel the *chiut* (divine life-force) of a rock, tree, or plant, approach the other slowly, expressing your gratitude.

2. Stop next to the other and ask permission to spend time together. If you feel something tight or constricted in your body

or your mind, say thanks, leave, and try another place or come back at a later time. If you feel nothing, or better yet, a sense of ease and spaciousness, continue on.

3. Extend your arms forward and to the side so that your open palms are facing the other. Move them forward and back from the other until you begin to sense the other's energy field, usually one to three feet away. When you're finished, say thanks and offer a blessing or prayer for the well-being of your partner.

You'll notice that the energy fields are weak around rocks and strong around plants, and off the charts around vegetation in the spring. Usually one hand is more energy sensitive than the other. For righties, it's usually the right hand, though for some (like me), the left is more sensitive.

Most people, myself included, feel downright silly when trying this practice the first few times. (Appendixes 1 and 2 address this issue.) If you discover your body's sensitivity to *chi* and *chiut*, you'll quickly get over it. But not everyone does. If this does not work for you, you should move on to other practices. When you return home, you might want to study with a teacher of Chi Quong or Tai Chi. Judith Orloff's book (see Resources) might also be helpful.

This exercise serves as the first step in the following two practices.

DRAWING THE DIVINE LIFE-FORCE FROM THE ELEMENTS

As a direct continuation of this previous exercise, we can explore the effect of specific elements on us by inviting their energy into our bodies.

I learned this technique as a Chi Quong exercise. The principle at play: where the mind goes, *chi* flows. Mental concentration and imagination make this body exercise work. It feels great because we are uniting our physical and spiritual aspects in one action. For those of us who tend to live in our heads, this practice truly overcomes the mind/body divide.

Practice 30
DRAWING *CHIUT* FROM THE ELEMENTS

1. Choose a part of the natural world whose energy you would like to experience. Favorite choices of mine include rivers, lakes or oceans, boulders, mountains, and the sky. (With living beings such as trees and flowers, practice 31 is preferable, as we send *chiut* back to them as well.)

2. After approaching and asking permission (see practice 29), focus your attention on the other.

3. Breathe in and out. Yogis suggest breathing through the nose; others prefer to breathe in through the nose, out through the mouth.

4. In your mind's eye, on the in-breath, image *chiut* streaming from your natural partner and entering your body. On the out-breath, mentally guide the *chiut* throughout your body and then into your heart. You can do this with eyes open or closed, whichever feels better. You might practice with palms extended as taught in practice 29, imaging the *chiut* passing through your hands.

The elements can have a powerful effect on your body and spirit. I am particularly enamored of water. I love to find a rock in the middle of a small creek where I can sit cross-legged, palms open and facing the current. Slow-moving water is relaxing. Granite boulders are grounding and mirror-like. Some elements, like copper, are like drinking a cup of coffee. (Ever been to Bisbee, Arizona, built around a copper mine?) Rock and boulders also serve as *chi* conduits, much like electrical conductors. Sit at the bottom of a long line of rocks, or on a massif of volcanic rock, and you might feel the charge of a power line.

EXCHANGING THE DIVINE LIFE-FORCE WITH A TREE

This is how my vision quest teacher, John Milton, taught us to exchange *chi* with a tree. I, of course, understand it as exchanging *chiut*, the divine energy that constitutes the *shefa*, the River of Light, that circulates through creation. This is the most tangible method I know for connecting to a Thou in the natural world.

Practice 31
EXCHANGE *CHIUT* WITH A TREE

1. Begin by standing a few yards from the tree. Admire its bark, leaves, or other features. Silently or out loud, tell the tree how beautiful it is.

2. Ask permission to approach, and if you feel relaxed rather than constricted, come closer and feel the tree's energy field with your outstretched arms and palms. All the while, you might tell the tree how you are feeling, expressing affection for your partner. You might adopt the Native American custom and call old trees grandmother or grandfather.

3. If you feel nothing constricting or tight, move close to the tree. Observe the patterns of the bark, notice if any insects are crawling along the surface, see if sap is oozing. All the while, share your feelings (admiration, joy, appreciation of beauty) with the tree.

4. Place your open palms on the tree. On the in-breath, breathe *chiut* from the tree through your hands into your body and heart, and then return *chiut* the same way on the out-breath.

The same technique can be used with any breathing entity in the natural world. Since wildlife won't sit still, however, it is generally used with trees, flowers, and other vegetation.

TEFILLIN AND CHIUT

A basic Chi Quong meditation involves standing with hands either at the side or cupped over the middle energy center (the *dam tiem*). On the in-breath, the mind's eye images *chi* streaming from the earth into the body through the feet and from the sky through the crown of the head. One can image roots extending from one's feet into the ground. This inspired the following practice with *tefillin*.

Wrapping oneself in *tefillin* is an age-old tradition (archaeologists have recovered *tefillin* from the time of the Bar Kochba revolt, 135 CE) that thoroughly involves the body. The *tefillin* consist of two small leather boxes tied on to the body by leather straps. Each contains portions of the Torah handwritten by a scribe on parchment (just like the Torah itself). Similar to a mezuzah, it holds key texts such as the *Sh'ma* and the *V'ahavta* from the prayer service. It is worn during the morning service, excepting Shabbat and holidays. Historically this ceremony was performed by men. Today, women are adopting it as well.

Practice 32
DRAWING *CHIUT* WITH TEFILLIN

1. Put on your *tefillin* in the normal way.[7] One of the *tefillin* boxes is placed on the crown of the head, facing the clouds. The other is wrapped around the arm, and it faces the heart.

2. Standing in a comfortable, upright posture, breathe in *chiut* from the sky through the upper *tefillin* box. Image the *chiut* traveling through your head, down the shoulder and into the arm, through the lower *tefillin* box, and into the heart. Notice the effect of the *chiut* on your heart.

3. If you like, chant Rabbi Shefa Gold's chant to the words one prays when laying *tefillin*. To my mind, it is one of the most beautiful and moving lines in the Hebrew Bible.

> *V'eirastich li l'olam, v'eirastich li b'tzedek uv'mishpat uv'chesed uv'rachamim, v'eirastich li be'emunah, v'yadat et Adonai.*
> I will betroth you to Me forever, I will betroth you to Me with righteousness, justice, loving-kindness, and compassion, I will betroth you to Me in trust/faith and you will know Adonai. (Hosea 2:21)[8]

Laying *tefillin* overcomes the Torah/nature divide, as the texts in the boxes and the body are joined in a tactile way. In this exercise, as in all meditations designed to facilitate the movement of *chiut*, the mind/body gap is obliterated as well.

I do not consider *tefillin* to be an amulet or talisman. I do believe that everything in the world has its own dynamic evolving *chiut*. A Torah text written by a scribe on parchment not only has symbolic value, but the special materials and sacred writing process create a different energy than the printing press. The *tefillin* both lends its *chiut* to our prayers and rituals and receives the *chiut* of all that interact with it, especially our prayers. Connected in the *shefa*, I also believe that one's individual set of phylacteries are affected by the Jews all over the world, and over the centuries, saying the same prayers with their *tefillin*. I do not think it is magic, but it feels magical, especially with *tefillin* handed down from one generation to the next.

FASTING IN WILDERNESS

For most people, the thought of fasting sends shivers down the spine. Now that I have completed several four-day fasts in wilderness, however, I have a different attitude. First let me clarify that I am speaking of fasting from food, and not water. **I do not advocate fasting from water in wilderness.**

The body is like an antenna for the *chi* and the *chiut* that flow through wilderness. For reasons I do not understand, when one fasts from food, the sensitivity of the body increases tenfold. I saw this quite tangibly on a solo retreat in the Chiricahua mountains of southern Arizona. Most people can see the aura around trees just as the sun is setting. The sky is lighter around the crowns as the trees become silhouettes in the darkening sky. One of my meditation practices was to lie on my back and watch the sky as the stars came out. Since the auras are not static—they stretch out and return like solar flares—they drew my attention. After two days of fasting, they were five to ten times bigger. The next day, after eating, they returned to normal.

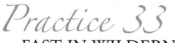

Practice 33
FAST IN WILDERNESS

1. Spend a morning, a day, or a few days in wilderness abstaining from food.

2. **Never jeopardize your safety by fasting.**

3. **Drink plenty of water.** This eliminates most hunger pains.

4. If you are feeling listless and wish to continue fasting, soak dry fruit in water and then drink the liquid. For a stronger beverage (this is too strong for some), mix the following into water and drink: cayenne pepper (for circulation), lemon (electrolytes), and molasses (slow-release sugar). Similarly, an electrolyte replacement drink such as Gatorade or Emer'gen-C can be used, but beware of a sugar rush and sudden energy drop-off afterwards.

5. Notice how your perception changes when fasting.

Most of us have issues with food, particularly a deep fear of suffering from its lack. I have done several four-day fasts now, so I can speak from experience. I only suffered hunger pains, on average, once during that time. When I studied for a week with noted tracker Tom Brown, Jr., he told us that he advises his students to fast the first day in wilderness, just to know that they don't need food. If subsequent tracking requires nonstop attention, they know they need not worry about a meal.

From the perspective of one's body, it is easier than you think. From the perspective of one's mind … I asked my vision quest teacher, John Milton, if I should fast during my first retreat with him. If it scares you, he said, that's a sign you need it. I fasted. He was right. Fasting is a tangible expression of yearning and surrender.

A Note on Yoga, Tai Chi, and Chi Quong

If you know one of these Eastern body practices, don't leave them at home. Any exercise that places mindful attention on the body is useful in spiritual wilderness practice, as it heightens our senses and thus our connection with the elements, plants, and animals around us. And if you are fasting, they help maintain one's energy level.

As mentioned above, Chi Quong directly connects one energetically with the rocks and trees and streams around us in the natural world. It helps us sensitize our bodies to the surrounding *chiut* and builds up our own energy levels as well. Chi Quong is a little easier in wilderness, as there are rarely flat surfaces for Yoga or Tai Chi. But having practiced them all, I recommend each as a beneficial supplement to Jewish spiritual practice in wilderness.

FOUR WINDS,
SEVEN DIRECTIONS

When morning comes ... the east wind awakens and
mercy prevails....

Zohar, Leviticus 23

"What have I got myself into?" I thought. My vision quest teacher, John Milton, was demonstrating a "four winds" ceremony. According to Native American teachings, each direction has certain qualities. The east (sunrise) contains the energy of birth and renewal; the west (sunset), transformation and death. Turn to the south (daylight) for life-force and rejuvenation; in the north (night) is universal wisdom. Milton taught us a Medicine Wheel, a map developed by Native Americans that locates the spirit-forces of the landscape. (There are many variations, as each tribe lived in a different place.)

He turned to the east and asked for the protection of all animals and beings to the east. He prayed for his students' renewal and a successful beginning to our solo retreat. When he finished, he threw a pinch of tobacco to the east. (Milton teaches: never come to the natural world only to take; we must also give. So an offering accompanied the prayer.) He continued in similar fashion to the south, west, and north. Then he prayed to father sky, throwing tobacco into the air. He buried a pinch of tobacco in the soil, praised mother earth, and asked for her continued support. Finally, he prayed to Great Spirit and sprinkled tobacco all around.

I thought to myself, "I'm a rabbi, I can't do this!" This is paganism. I was trying to keep an open mind, but nothing in Judaism comes close to this kind of ritual and the theological thinking behind it ... then I felt like I had been hit by a sledge-hammer. That's not true, of course. I do something incredibly sim-ilar every year! On Sukkot, I take the four species—palm frond (*lulav*), citrus fruit (*etrog*), myrtle branch (*hadas*), willow branch (*aravah*)—and wave them in the four directions, and then up and down to sky and earth.

For a while, I just sat stunned. Then I realized: of course I can try this ceremony. Recall that the kabbalists and the Hasidim teach that God enters the world as a *shefa* and that this divine River of Light breaks into streams and tributaries (the ten spheres or aspects of God) that interact with the world in different ways, yet come from the One. As long as I viewed the four winds as manifestations of the one God (what scholars of Jewish mysticism call *panen*the-ism as opposed to the *pan*theism of the pagans), I was on solid ground. In fact, by praying in a seventh direction, to Great Spirit, Milton had already incorporated the monotheistic viewpoint.

Returning home, I began to look for Jewish sources and other rit-uals that incorporated a similar approach. Mystical literature, I knew, had a rich variety of understandings and symbols for the physical world. Was there something like a Jewish Medicine Wheel? Little did I know that another rabbi was already engaged in the same search.

RABBI GERSHON WINKLER AND A JEWISH MEDICINE WHEEL

Gershon Winkler's journey could only have happened in America. An ultra-Orthodox rabbi in New York, he left the pious life for the Wild West, working on ranches as a cowpoke. Eventually he set-tled on pristine land near Cuba, New Mexico, where he integrates his love of Judaism with wilderness spirituality at his nonprofit organization, the Walking Stick Foundation. He is reviving the magical side of Kabbalah, retrieving and re-creating a Jewish shamanic practice.

In his book, *Magic of the Ordinary: Recovering the Shamanic in Judaism,* Winkler indeed constructs a Jewish Medicine Wheel. In chapter 3, "The Wheel of the Four Winds," Winkler draws on a wide range of Jewish sources: Bible, Midrash (scriptural interpretation), and mystical literature.[1] He contributes his own midrash, interpreting the meanings of the directions according to the etymology of their Hebrew names. Some of the Medicine Wheel he improvises himself, filling in the gaps when the sources are incomplete. While he does not like to admit (and take the credit he deserves for) the fact that he sometimes develops rather than recovers traditions, I believe that this kind of creativity, itself firmly rooted in Jewish tradition, is needed to return Judaism to wilderness. Winkler offers us an astute synthesis of ancient and contemporary thinking on the four winds in Judaism, a portion of which I summarize below. In fleshing out a Jewish Medicine Wheel for use in Jewish wilderness practice, some of my own insights have naturally crept in. See *Magic of the Ordinary* for a pure rendering of Rabbi Winkler's thought.

A JEWISH MEDICINE WHEEL

A Medicine Wheel is a map. For the Native Americans, each direction is the spirit home of certain animals. Particular colors, elements, and spirit beings are also associated with the directions. These associations become part of a story—our story—of birth (east), life (south), death (west), gestation (north), and rebirth (east again, as the cycle repeats).[2] As we shall see below, this narrative opens up new areas for spiritual practice in wilderness. In particular, we can pray for the spiritual qualities that are associated with each direction.

In biblical and rabbinic literature, angels were considered discreet, corporeal beings with specific qualities, talents, and/or tasks, lending each its own special character. In line with the mystical theology discussed above, I consider them particular parts of the *shefa*, that is, as impersonal but real aspects of God's dynamic energy pulsing through the world.

EAST

Hebrew name: *kedem* (beginning, before); *mizrach* (shine)

Spirit-energy: Gavriel (strong man of God); *chesed* (lovingkindness)

Animal: Lion

Element: Air

Kedem means "before," an appropriate name for the direction of the sunrise, and symbolizes beginnings. The element of the east, air, is a direct reference to birth in Hebrew culture. In the form of the breath, air is the instrument through which God gives life to humans and animals. The east, then, is the place of renewal, a source of hope.

The other name for east, *mizrach*, denotes "shining." Light shines on us at sunrise and illuminates our lives. It enables us to see clearly, to distinguish the various entities on the earth.

To begin again is no simple matter. It often requires courage (the lion) and strength (Gavriel). In kabbalistic parlance, Gavriel is also the force of balance, the disciplining of strength. Successful births benefit from inner balance, from sound judgment and emotional stability.

When the wind blows from the east, or when facing the east, particularly at sunrise, we might express gratitude for light, warmth, and hope, for the promise of a new day. We can pray for clarity of vision, courage, strength, and balance. According to a passage in the Zohar,

God's compassion enters the world at dawn with the east wind. We might pray for chesed, *God's loving-kindness, however little we might think we merit it.*

SOUTH

Hebrew name: *negev* (cleanse, wipe); *darom* (of heights)

Spirit-energy: Michael (who is like God?)

Animal: human

Element: fire

The south also has two names, both related to the great Negev desert south of Beersheva in the Land of Israel. It has high mountains (near the present-day border between Israel and Egypt, south of Gaza). But for the most part, the Negev is a great plain, where mountains have been "wiped away."

The south is where the human goes for cleansing, to wipe the slate clean. It is the direction of *teshuvah*. We cannot hide, even from ourselves—especially from ourselves. Exposed in the full light of day, we can best see our egos, our sense of "I," in the south. We can appreciate our individuality and then subject it to the kind of rational analysis that sees through self-deception. Michael is the force of reflection. This is the spiritual energy we invoke in solitude, when we seek to discover our true selves. Like Elijah, we travel south, alone, leaving all past achievements, titles, and wealth behind, to hear the "still, small voice" (1 Kings 19:12).

Teshuvah is anything but fun. We must suffer the pain of seeing our problematic selves as we really are. Without fire, without a passion to be better and different, it would be impossible.

When the wind blows from the south, or when facing the south, particularly during the day, we can express gratitude for the special, unique persons that we are, for our mental abilities, and for our malleable natures—our capacity to change. We might pray for the elements of teshuvah: *a clear, undistorted vision of the person I am, a vision of the person I need to become, and a passion for the difficult process of growth and change. We can fashion new goals and resolve to carry them through.*

WEST

Hebrew name: *ma'arav* (blending, merging, mixing)

Spirit-energy: Rafael (God has healed)

Animal: bull

Element: earth

Ma'arav, "blending," is an apt description of light and dark at sunset. As the light fades and we can no longer stand out as an individual, we lose our distinct sense of self. The west brings up endings and death. We merge into we, into community; we merge into the earth, into death.

The west, teaches Rabbi Winkler, is the home of the healing spirit-force, Rafael, because here we encounter the obstacles that we must overcome if we are to heal: the fear of death in general and the fear of our own mortality in particular. The bull or buffalo resides in the west because it is a herd animal; it merges with its fellows. But the bull is also known for its strength and tenacious, unrelenting effort. Against all odds, the bull pushes forward. It does not waver in the face of death.

Despite the fact that sunset and autumn are metaphors for endings and death, sunset is the beginning of the Jewish day, and autumn is the beginning of the new year. This points to one of the paradoxical realities of living in this world. Birth actually begins with death. Just as the seed must die to allow a sapling to emerge, parts of us must die if we are to change and grow. This is why, according to one mainstream interpretation, we rehearse our deaths by fasting and wearing white, the color of the Jewish funeral shroud, on the autumn holiday Yom Kippur. We facilitate the death of our bad character traits.

In autumn, the leaves die. But another reality is also evident. The tree is letting go, preparing itself for renewed growth in the spring. So too with us. In the west, we learn to let go, so that we may later rebirth ourselves in the east, at sunrise, and in the spring.

Ma'arav, therefore, is also the place of gelling, the place of wisdom and understanding, where life's lessons are understood and processed so that we might move forward. The earth not only accepts the dead, she recycles them, preparing them for life in new form.

When the wind blows from the west, or when facing the west, especially at sunset, we might express gratitude for our lives, our triumphs as well as our tragedies. We can say thanks for our mistakes. Here we seek healing, through prayer and letting go. We can pray for steadfast courage to face our fears of death. We can ask for patience in the face of uncertainty, for when we let go of parts of ourselves, we do not know what we will become. After all, we still have to pass the mystery that lies to the north before we are reborn in the east. Finally, we can ask for wisdom to understand the stories that are our lives. May we learn the lessons of our failures. As we climb into the cocoon and head into the darkness, we may pray that our potential be realized, so that one day we may emerge a beautiful new butterfly.

NORTH

Hebrew name: *tzafon* (hidden)

Spirit-energy: Uriel (God is my light)

Animal: eagle

Element: water

Between death and rebirth, we encounter the mystery of our existence. It is in the darkness of the womb that life is conceived.

As water comes from snow, its connection to the north is grounded in geography—if you live in the northern hemisphere. But on this Jewish Medicine Wheel, of course, it is also a metaphor. Water nourishes a seed, catalyzing it to release its shell and become a seedling. Water fills the womb. Water symbolizes the fluid energy of erosion, conception, and gestation that enables birth.

Most interesting, the name Uriel comes from *or* (light). It is in the mysterious darkness that we gain illumination. We live in the information age, but when it comes to the important things in life, we know so little. We know much about the mechanics of the natural world, but we cannot fathom how the beauty and majesty of this earth are even possible. Yet it is when we suffer what Heschel called our "higher incomprehension"[3] that we might be enlightened. We are not lifted by factual knowledge, but by God's unfathomable yet real presence.

The eagle is known for the reclusive, hidden places that it nests. But in Jewish sources, the eagle's wings, so effective in shielding its offspring, are a symbol for God's immanence and protection as well.[4] Somehow the mystery is not to be feared, but loved. It does not send us hatred, but compassion. This world is good, despite the darkness, despite the partial death we have suffered in the west, for we trust that the dawn will soon follow.

The north, then, is the place of yearning, the place of faith, the place we must fight our demons and fears that we are unworthy of rebirth. The north is where we tremble, hoping we are capable of change. Mirroring the south as a place to seek vision, the north is where we listen in the dark for new inspiration and fresh ideas as to what we might become.

Facing the north, particularly at night while looking to the stars, we might express gratitude for the fact that there is a world, and human beings on it, at all. Fully realizing just how little our spot in the universe is, we might say thanks for the fact that we can make a difference in the world. We might ask for a vision, a direction and purpose for our lives. We might pray to understand the hidden parts of our subconscious that baffle us, for the patience and strength to be reborn, for the ability to change. We might seek connection to the great mystery, asking for shelter under the divine wings, praying for intimacy with God.

UP

While the last two directions are much less developed in Jewish sources, they too are part of a Jewish Medicine Wheel. Rabbi Winkler assigns the *tzome'ach*, "plants," to this direction, for they grow up toward the sky. And looking skyward, we see the vastness of the universe. We are reminded of transcendence and eternity, just as the Jewish people looked up to Mount Sinai. We are reminded of the future, the part of our lives that waits for us just beyond the horizon.[5]

Finally, it is the transcendent aspect of God that grounds our ethics.[6] Looking upward calls to mind the ethical injunctions we received at Sinai, which can be summed up with the later commandment, "Justice, justice, shall you pursue!" (Deut. 16:20).

Looking upward, we are thankful for God's transcendence, for the kedushah *in the world and the* kedushah *in us. We can express gratitude for our ability to discriminate between right and wrong. The unlimited sky reminds us of the unlimited possibilities that we humans enjoy. We might be grateful for human freedom and pray for our future.*

We might ask for justice: for ourselves, for humanity, for the planet.

DOWN

Feeling the earth against our feet, we experience God's immanence, the *Shechinah*, and recall the immediate relations in our lives. Facing downward, we recognize mother earth: our home and our support, the womb of all life. Down is the direction of the *domem*, the still ones, that is, the elements, the building blocks of life that compose the earth. Our bodies are part of her body. And it is in our bodies, in the relations with those around us, that we know love.[7]

We are reminded of that which is hidden from us below, where we have been but can no longer go, the past.[8]

Looking down, we can say thanks for God's presence in the here and now, in the sensuous earth. We might express gratitude for our bodies and this messy, sweaty, wonderful life. Here is where spiritual life is possible; here is where love lives.

Perhaps kneeling and placing our hands on the ground, we can pray for stability. We might pray for the health of mother earth, her creatures and features, and make our vows to prevent her undue exploitation by humankind. We might pray for love and intimacy with our fellow creatures, and with God.

CONNECTING INNER AND OUTER GEOGRAPHY

Four winds ceremonies are a powerful way to connect inner and outer geography. In the following practice, our hearts extend into the natural world as we direct our prayers toward God's presence in specific parts of wilderness.

As discussed in appendix 2, the prohibition against idolatry is a real concern in this and other practices in *A Wild Faith*. When we pray toward the east, for instance, we must be careful to differentiate between the beings, forces, and qualities of the east and God, lest we identify God solely with the natural world. This is subtle, as I follow Jewish mystics and Martin Buber in locating divinity *in* the natural world. To stay clear of this confusion, then, I am careful to pray to the divine in nature as opposed to the mountains or a spirit-force, even though I do address them in the following four winds ceremony. So while I may ask for the protection of all the beings in the east, or ask the spirit-force of the north for illumination, I direct my prayer to God. I do this by addressing God's immanence in the world, the aspect of God the kabbalists named the *Shechinah*. So when I ask, say, for enlightenment from Uriel, I address this energy as a child of the *Shechinah* (see practice 34).

Do this practice immediately after choosing a Soul-O site or a campsite, before unpacking gear and settling in. In fact, the ceremony is a way of discerning if this is an appropriate site for your practice. If you feel constricted or cold during the ceremony, you should move on (unless you are dealing with issues of death and rebirth; I spent my last solo retreat in such a site).

Practice 34
FOUR WINDS, SEVEN DIRECTIONS GRATITUDE AND PERMISSION CEREMONY

1. Stand in the center of your site, facing to the east. Take a deep breath, calm yourself, and listen. As in meditative walking (practice 2), place a quarter of your attention on the breath, a quarter on the feel of your feet against the ground, and half on the world around you. Take in all that you are sensing.

2. Express gratitude and pray for the wellness of all beings who live in the east. For instance, you might say, "To all *b'nei haShechinah bamizrach* [children of the *Shechinah* in the east], home of renewal and courage and hope, may you live in peace. May you be protected from all harm. I thank you for the light and warmth you give, for the hope you plant in my heart. Thank you for all you bring to the world, for all the *kedushah* you hold in God's creation, for your presence here in the *Shechinah* and the *Shechinah* in you. Thank you for being here with me today."

3. Ask for permission to be in this place, and the protection of the beings to the east. "*B'nei haShechinah bamizrach* [pray in English if you are unsure of the Hebrew], I ask your permission

| | | In Prayer, Ask for: | | | | In Prayer, Offer Gratitude for: |
Direction	Hebrew Name	Spirit-Energy	Animal	Element	Qualities	
East	*Kedem* (beginning, before) *Mizrach* (shine)	Gavriel Strength Balance	Lion Courage	Air Breath Life	Birth Renewal *Chesed* (lovingkindness)	Light Warmth Hope
South	*Negev* (cleanse, wipe) *Darom* (of heights)	Michael Sound thinking Self-clarity	Human Creativity	Fire Passion	Clarity Set personal goals Resolve to accomplish goals	Individuality Rational thought Capacity to change
West	*Ma'arav* (blending, merging)	Rafael Healing of body Healing of emotional wounds	Bull Persistence Fearlessness	Earth Death Recycling	Death Merging: community Gelling: wisdom and understanding Realization of personal potential	Accomplishments Failures and mistakes
North	*Tzafon* (hidden)	Uriel Illumination Personal vision	Eagle Protection Freedom	Water Change	Mystery Yearning for birth and intimacy with the Divine Faith/trust in God and universe Strength to identify and fight subconscious demons	The universe Life
Up		God's Transcendence	*Tzome'ach* Growing things		Possibility Future	Idealism Justice
Down		God's Immanence	*Domem* Still things (elements)		Stability Past	My body Love

to stay in this place. I ask for your protection from all harm, physical and emotional, as I practice in service to God. May my practice benefit you and all creation."

4. Ask for the gifts of the east in your spiritual practice. "Please
God, may I be granted strength and balance this day. May I enjoy
your *chesed*. May your light help me to see the challenges before
me in renewing my life." Try to be specific. "Please God, grant
me courage to face my fear of _____ or my difficulty with
_____ during my practice today" or, "May it be your
will, *Ruach ha'olam* [Spirit of the world], that I find the right
direction in my work or relationship and find a way to begin
again with my boss or significant other."

5. Repeat to the south, west, north, up, and down, evoking the
qualities of each direction. You might kneel and touch the
ground when thanking the earth. You may prefer to do this exercise barefoot to feel the earth.

6. If you are in the southern hemisphere, substitute the qualities of
the north for the south and vice versa. Travel the Medicine Wheel
in counterclockwise direction.

7. Take your time. After your prayers in a given direction, enter
receptive mode and listen for a possible response.

8. Finally, turning to the seventh direction (everywhere), offer gratitude and ask protection from the *Shechinah*, from God. You may
want to rotate slowly during your prayer, as God is all around. You
might try offering this prayer with your eyes closed, connecting to
the landscape and listening for God with your other senses.

9. Be creative. Be playful in your prayer and see how that affects your
relation with God and wilderness. If you are in particular need of
something, stay in the appropriate direction and pray for it. If your
courage is waning, face the east and ask for lion energy. If you

need to work on a personal issue, request the help of Michael's gifts while facing the south. If you are emotionally out of balance or physically sick, ask Rafael for healing while facing the west.

Sacrifice, of course, was the heart of ancient Israelite religion, and I have to say, throwing something tangible into the wind with one's prayers, like sage or tobacco, is a powerful practice. It feels great to actually give something to the land we stand on. But we Jews substituted prayer for sacrifice some two thousand years ago, when our own sacrificial service was abruptly ended by the Roman destruction of the Temple in Jerusalem. Keeping with the spirit of Jewish tradition, therefore, I let my prayer, no small thing either, suffice as the offering in four winds ceremony.

The four winds, seven directions ceremony is an important Soul-O site practice. When in multiday retreat, I practice it every morning and evening.

SUKKOT AND THE FOUR WINDS

The previous practice can be adapted to the traditional Jewish four winds ceremony, the waving of the four species on the Jewish holiday of Sukkot. As we head into winter, we might ask that the qualities of each of the directions germinate within us.

Practice 35
THE FOUR SPECIES AND THE FOUR WINDS

1. Perform the mitzvah of waving the four species in the normal manner.[9]

2. As you wave your four species, ask to receive the divine energy that is associated with each direction. For instance, while waving the *lulav* to the east, pray for and/or visualize the energy of mercy and renewal.

3. As part of the waving the four species, draw the qualities into your heart by pulling the four species into your chest at the end of each shaking.

An additional four winds practice, for *teshuvah*, may be found in chapter 13 (practice 43).

Four winds, seven directions ceremonies have become a major component of my spiritual practice in wilderness. I find it a powerful tool in many areas of spiritual practice: listening to wild nature, gratitude, yearning, *teshuvah*. But there is room for caution in working with a Medicine Wheel.

THE PROBLEM WITH MEDICINE WHEELS

A Medicine Wheel translates the experience of the natural world into a set of symbols. Like any language, it can take on a reality of its own. There is a real danger that instead of leading us to their source, wild nature, the symbols only reflect our preconceived notions about the natural world back at us. A Medicine Wheel can blind us to the reality of the land right before our eyes.

This need not be the case, but it is hard to avoid. In addition to the problem of living in our own symbolic universe rather than wild nature, there are two additional obstacles that must be overcome.

First, the road to the subconscious is through images and their symbolic meanings. To translate nature's qualities into words and symbols can be appropriate, especially when we are working with our subconscious selves, that is, when we are doing *teshuvah*. But when we engage the natural world to tell us about our psyches, we are manipulating nature for our own purposes. In the language of Martin Buber, it becomes an It. We are not turning to the natural world as an asymmetrical but equal partner, a real entity with its own needs irrespective of its value to us as a mirror of our unconscious. We are not entering into relation with a Thou to whom we must listen deeply, without knowing the outcome in advance. In genuine relation, we serve our Thou; the Thou does not serve us.[10]

Second, a Medicine Wheel is the product of a local geography. Some experiences of nature are universal. Across the world, people will likely associate the east with birth and the west with death. But after that, we have to recognize that the actual experience of the natural world is always local. Everything that the north symbolizes in the northern hemisphere lies to the south in the southern hemisphere. Fall is different in New England than in southern California. Water may symbolize the same thing for two different cultures, but which direction is aligned with water might have to do with the direction of the nearest ocean. Indeed, a second name for west in Hebrew is *yama* (literally "seaward"), referring to the Mediterranean Sea's location relative to the Land of Israel. This is why Native American Medicine Wheels differ from tribe to tribe.[11] The Jewish Medicine Wheel presented here is connected to the Land of Israel.[12] Its relevance to other landscapes should not be assumed.

How do we overcome these obstacles? I offer three suggestions.

Put I-It Interactions into an I-Thou Context—Martin Buber never thought that we could live our entire lives in I-Thou relation. He knew that we live most of our lives in I-It. We need not deny that. Rather, we should let I-Thou moments provide the context for I-It. There is a place for symbolic thinking in spiritual practice, as long as it is part of a balanced relationship, in which we relate to the natural world primarily as a Thou.

Turn the It into a Thou—Let the symbolic put you into dialogue with the natural world. This is why it is important to start with mindfulness and gratitude practices. We begin by addressing the natural phenomena that gave rise to the symbolic language in the first place. We say "You" to our potential

Thou. (More on this topic in appendix 2.) Then, as in any dialogue, we can listen. When you turn to the east and pray for renewal, wait for a response before you move on to the south. When you turn to the south to ask for clarity in self-understanding, listen and see what comes up. Enter receptive mode before returning to words.

Trust Your Own Experience—If your meditation or prayer in a given direction evokes qualities other than those in this Jewish Medicine Wheel, give priority to your own perception. A Medicine Wheel is a means to connect us to God in the natural world. If it isn't working for you in your particular environment, use the Jewish Medicine Wheel as an example rather than a blueprint for the connection between inner and outer geography. Find your own connection. Turn to the sky, the earth, or a specific direction, and just listen. See what the natural world evokes in your heart. Respond with personal prayer.

When used skillfully, a Jewish Medicine Wheel is a welcome tool for Jewish spiritual practice in wilderness.

TESHUVAH: THE WILD
HEART OF REPENTANCE

> Repentance is like the ocean … the ocean is always open, and likewise the gates of repentance are always open. Whenever you wish to bathe in the ocean, you can do so. So with repentance—whenever you wish to repent, God will receive you.
>
> **Rabbi Samuel ben Nachman[1]**

At first glance, *teshuvah* (repentance) practices seem antithetical to the spirit of this book, as they direct our attention away from the natural world. To do *teshuvah*, we shine the spotlight of awareness on our personalities. We look inward and enter receptive mode to directly receive our own selves. But of course, it is yin to yang, the opposite bookend to mindfulness in a wholesome spiritual practice.

Teshuvah and *cheit* (sin) are somewhat less judgmental in the Hebrew than their English translations. *Cheit* is an archery term; its literal meaning is "to miss the mark." It presumes good rather than bad intentions on the part of the person who sins. The method of improving one's aim is *teshuvah*, which literally means "turning." Repentance is turning and returning to the mark, to God. So in fact, we have been doing *teshuvah* all along. Any moment of I-Thou is a moment of *teshuvah*.

Unlike the previous practices in *A Wild Faith*, *teshuvah* practices are mental and analytical. Particularly during High Holy Days, we are urged to examine our lives, identify where we need to improve, and resolve to do something about it. But *teshuvah* requires more of us than good thinking, and that is why practicing *teshuvah* in wilderness can make all the difference in the world.

TESHUVAH IN WILDERNESS

Critiquing oneself accurately and honestly invariably involves a change in perspective—a new vantage point from which to see oneself with some dispassion and objectivity. This can happen anytime we break our routine and have some time to reflect. To some degree, any vacation will do. But wilderness supports *teshuvah* in ways that other locations cannot.

Enter the backcountry and we have not only left our routines; we have left civilization behind. Away from the constructs that support our usual lives, we enter a world without job, traffic, advertising, sports, restaurants, gardening, chores, movies, the Internet, and talk radio. It is readily apparent just how much of our "civilized" lives are based on human conventions and inventions. And with that realization comes its corollary, the fundamental assumption of *teshuvah*: what has been constructed can be deconstructed.

No longer in the environment that elicits our habitual responses, with little to defend, our social selves become transparent. Our personalities are exposed in wilderness. We see how easy it is to be a different kind of person. I have always marveled at the fact that I rarely encounter a selfish, mean-spirited person while backpacking. It could be that backpacking attracts certain personality types, but I'm convinced that wilderness brings out a person's virtues rather than shortcomings. One sees how much we humans subconsciously invent ourselves. So much of what seems to be immutable reality is really a choice.

GETTING HONEST WITH YOURSELF

I suppose there is something harder to achieve in the world than self-honesty, but I don't know what it is. I'm astonished by the lengths we go to avoid looking clearly at who we are. Why? For one thing, we'd rather avoid the unpleasantness and pain. For another, it's hard to figure out what really motivates our actions.

Still, we must try.

It's almost always worth the effort. Even when we do not change as much as we'd like, we still access something incredible when doing *teshuvah*: the deep joy that only comes from getting real and living in truth. Often the tears are flowing and the heart is hurting, but it feels right anyway, for there is no stronger bedrock on which to stand than knowing the truth about ourselves. Living in truth, we can trust that things will get better. Living in denial, we remain captive to whatever wound we have endured, stuck in whatever web our lies to ourselves have spun. It takes energy to deceive ourselves and pretend we do not need to mourn, learn, let go, and go forward. When we embrace the pain of our failures and the wounds inflicted by others, it hurts, but we know we are moving on.

LET WILDERNESS CHANGE YOU

The process of *teshuvah* is different for me when living in wilderness. I used to ask God to help me change in ways that I feared I could not. Indeed, I didn't. Now I sense that if I can connect myself to God's good world, physically as well as spiritually, the grip of my bad habits loosens. As I am drawn by the experience of awe in the natural world, I become the kind of person who lives in receptive mode and experiences I-Thou. Rather than dwelling in guilt about my bad traits, I am pulled toward new paradigms and possibilities.

Teshuvah is never easy. But in wilderness—where I feel the earth holding me, where I know possibility is as tangible as the horizon, where my heart soars—*teshuvah* is more doable than I ever imagined.

PRACTICES

The following practices are divided into three sections that represent stages in the process of *teshuvah*:

1. Get Still—Think about your life from a place of mindfulness.

2. Be Honest—In examining your life, don't hold back. Be ruthless.

3. Share It—Express your yearning, share your pain, and set your intention to change.

To do a "*teshuvah* session" in wilderness, start with 1, then choose a practice from 2, and conclude with a practice from 3. **If you are suffering from any kind of psychological ailment, do not do these practices alone in wilderness without consulting your therapist or doctor.** Living in wilderness requires sound judgment, and safety demands our constant attention. **The best way to avoid accidents and bad weather is to remain aware of one's surroundings and think ahead.** While we hope to engage our emotions fully, we must be sure that they do not impair our decisions or occupy our attention so completely that we put ourselves at risk.

1. GET STILL

Stilling the Mind and Listening Within

Most people (rightly) think of self-examination when they hear the word *teshuvah*, but the chances for successful *teshuvah* are lessened when we forget its actual meaning: turning to God. If all it took to change was to identify our problems, we'd all be much better people already. Rather, personal growth requires discipline and resolve, the ability to suffer the pain of examining our vices, and the courage to risk giving up the defense mechanisms that shield us. The strength and inspiration one gains from a real relationship with God are more than helpful. Before we analyze our personalities, we need to see the holy potential in ourselves. And as mentioned above, thinking from a place of mindfulness—emotionally calm, open, and nonjudgmental—cuts through the clutter of our egoism.

Living in receptive mode, then, has an enormous effect on our ability to do *teshuvah.* The previous practices in this book are not independent of *teshuvah.* Rather, connecting to God makes *teshuvah* possible.

> Find a place of calm and stillness using one of the meditative methods we have learned previously—such as following the breath (practice 11), chanting (practice 27), repeating a phrase (practice 23), or meditative walking (practice 2).

Generally, when thoughts arise, the instruction is to let them go. When working with our thinking minds in *teshuvah* exercises, however, we may be searching for just the insight that our subconscious sends our way when we free ourselves from our usual thought patterns. If a feeling or thought comes that seems to be important, hold it in your awareness. Rest with it. You will be tempted to begin an analysis: describing the problem, making lists, eliminating false leads, and otherwise thinking deductively. For the most part, though, try to avoid logical thinking. Rather, breathe, and just be with it. See how it feels in your body. Listen for what it wants to tell you.

When you are ready, proceed to a practice in section 2.

2. BE HONEST

Speaking Truth to Self
Telling the truth about ourselves, to ourselves, just might be the hardest thing we are ever asked to do. Yet it is so important. This

is the heart of *teshuvah*, finding our way to our best selves through self-awareness and gentle self-criticism.

My teacher Sylvia Boorstein begins many a teaching with the simple question, "What's true?" Whatever the topic, she asks: Am I actually getting at the truth, or am I really rationalizing my past behavior, defending my self-esteem, speaking from anger or jealousy, or just being too lazy to think it through?

Practice 36
WHAT'S TRUE

1. In your journal, write a question about yourself that begins, "What's true...?" For example, you might write about recurring themes in your life, such as, "What's true about how I relate to people?" or "What's true about how I react to X or Y?" You can ask directly about your personality traits, such as "What's true about me vis-à-vis arrogance/humility, assertive/passive, lazy/disciplined, and so on?" Or you might ask, "What's true about the way I ... receive love, give love, make friends, respond to friends' problems, listen to my children, prioritize my activities, make the world a better place, and the like?" Choose things that are important in your life.

2. Alternatively, if something is troubling you about a relationship with your partner, child, parent, or friend, you might ask, "What's true?" about the situation.

3. Do not immediately start writing. Rather, breathe. Just be with it. Focus on what you see around you, or the sensations of your body, and wait ... for whatever comes up. It might be quite different than what you would have normally thought.

4. Write down what comes to mind without judgment, as if in a "brainstorming" session. You can always analyze your thoughts later.

5. Journal your thoughts about what needs to change in your life.

So…what's true?

Talking to God—Rabbi Nachman's *Hitbodedut*

This is the practice that Rabbi Nachman of Breslov made famous. With some latitude, I translate *hitbodedut* as "alone time for spiritual purpose." While you can do it anywhere, Rabbi Nachman, aware of the supportive flow of *chiut* in natural settings, preferred the natural world.

Practice 37
HITBODEDUT

1. Find a place of solitude in wilderness.

2. Talk out loud to God for a set period of time (not less than twenty minutes) and don't stop. A stopwatch or alarm is helpful so that you won't think about the time. Rabbi Nachman is said to have devoted an hour.

3. Speak, ask, figure things out, pray—whatever comes up, share it with God.

This practice can be difficult at first, but getting over the inhibition of talking out loud to God is not particularly hard. Rather, the problem is that you will quickly run out of things to say. But you must keep speaking. This is where it gets interesting. You will find yourself saying things that you had no idea were in you. In psychological terms, you have cleared room for your subconscious to send whatever it needs you to know into the light of day.

As in any exercise where we zero in on what is truly happening in our hearts and what we really need, personal prayer is an appropriate conclusion.

Writing to God

In this journal practice, we address God directly.

Practice 38
WRITE A LETTER TO GOD

1. In a wilderness spot, still the mind, and listen within. Take in the natural world.

2. When you are ready, open your journal. Write the most honest thing you can to God. You might describe your wishes for yourself or for your family and friends. You might write about the things you need most. You might ask for guidance.

3. Alternatively, you might consider writing your letter in the spirit of Rabbi Nachman of Breslov's practice of *hitbodedut*. I don't know if Julia Cameron had heard of Rabbi Nachman when she made this a core exercise in her book, *The Artist's Way,* but it is the same idea. Open your journal and begin to write. The only rule: don't stop to think; just write and do not quit. Before you begin, set the number of journal pages that you will fill. You'll want to write for at least twenty minutes and probably not more than an hour. Cameron recommends three 8½- x 11-inch ruled pages. You will run out of things to say, but you must keep writing. Soon enough, previously hidden ideas and feelings will make their appearance.

Whatever comes up, share it with God in your letter. You might conclude with a prayer for what you need and gratitude for what you have.

Hike with a Question
To receive an answer, it helps to ask a question. In fact, a good question is already half the answer.

Practice 39
CARRY A QUESTION

1. Walk, hike, kayak, or ski mindfully with a question or concern you need to address.

2. You can write the question in your journal as a reminder or on a piece of paper that you keep in your pocket.

3. Your question might concern a major issue in your life: an important relationship, a recurring pattern, or a personality trait you would like to change.

4. Before you begin to move with your question, set an intention: "Please God, may I gain insight into my question during the course of the day." Then let it go.

5. Every half hour or so, remind yourself of the question, but refrain from analyzing it. Rather, keep listening for insight. (You'll forget for hours at a time, but that's okay. It will reappear when it's ready.)

6. If appropriate, write what you learn in your journal, and comment on it at the end of the day.

This is a somewhat delicate exercise, as we don't think about our problem deliberately while hiking; rather we seek the fruits of mindfulness that come from body awareness and staying in the present. We carry the question like a necklace, always there, but not the focus of our attention.

As the day progresses, see if a new insight or a different perspective emerges.

Converse with the People in Your Life
The mitzvah or commandment of *teshuvah* directs us to seek forgiveness from, and to reconcile with, the people in our lives. Often we struggle with how to do this. We might also be baffled by how we came to the current state of affairs that require redress. What was/is truly motivating our actions toward each other?

Though we are alone in wilderness, in this practice we open a dialogue by inviting people to join us for a conversation. If you are familiar with the practice of *ushpizin*, welcoming honored guests such as Abraham and David to join us in the Sukkah on Sukkot in spirit rather than body, you already have experience in this exercise. Night is a good time for this practice, as it is easier to visualize a guest in the darkness. Some people enjoy doing it while tending a campfire; the light of a full moon works for me.

Practice 40
TESHUVAH DIALOGUE

1. Find a secluded place, or sit in your Soul-O site.

2. Invite a person with whom you would like to speak. It can be a friend, a coworker, a relative. A great advantage of this practice is that you can dialogue with a person who has passed away. Invoke their presence by calling their name; welcome them to this place.

3. Through writing in your journal or speaking out loud, say what you need to say to this person. You might speak about past events, express your feelings toward them, ask forgiveness. You might ask a question.

4. Get still, listen, and imagine their response. Write it down, or speak it out loud.

5. Then respond.

The dialogue can go on for five minutes or all night.[2]

Ask Your Death

Our personalities are always in flux as we change and evolve. While it's easy to focus on the new, it's important to remember that adopting one attitude or behavior often entails stopping another. In many cases, it is like a gate at the airport. The arriving jet cannot unload its passengers before the previous one takes off. Sometimes the way to midwife a new beginning is to concentrate on an ending. What part of my personality needs to die for a new me to emerge? (See the discussion of the west wind in chapter 12.)

Wear your death on your shoulder, say the Buddhists. Rabbi Eliezer taught, "Repent one day before you die" (*Pirkei Avot* 2:15), meaning, consider every day as if it were your last. This is good advice not only because, indeed, tomorrow might be one's last day. Rather, we are so seduced by the trials and tribulations of the moment, we rarely attain the truest perspective we have—the perspective of a whole life. So if you want to figure out the right thing to do in a given situation, ask your death.[3] The following exercises require us to break through the taboos of our Western culture, which frowns upon realistic talk of death. But the rewards are enormous: a better ability to, in the famous words of Deuteronomy (39:19), "choose life!"

Practice 41
WRITE YOUR OWN EULOGY

This is Tom Sawyer practice. Tom, you might recall, attended his own funeral. In this exercise, we try to better understand our lives by imagining how others see us.

1. In your journal, write the eulogy that you would like to hear at a memorial service to mark your life. You might talk about the personality traits your friends loved in you or some of the more memorable things that you did. You might write about how you led a life of service. Your eulogy can be long or short.

2. Ask yourself a tough question. Were your funeral held today, would you likely hear the things in your eulogy? What would be different? Try to be as specific as possible. Write down your answer.

3. Write your *teshuvah* to-do list. What things do you need to do differently in order to merit the eulogy you wrote? What part of you needs to die?

Practice 42
LIE IN YOUR GRAVE

An extraordinary midrash reads:

> Every year on the ninth of Av, for all those years that Israel was in the desert, Moses would announce among the camp: "Go out and dig." The people would then dig graves and lie down in them. In the morning Moses would announce: "The living shall be separated from the dead."[4]

The Israelites were commanded to confront their own deaths in the most concrete of ways!

1. After the sun goes down, pick a safe, secluded spot.

2. Lie down on the earth and imagine that you are lying in your own grave. How does it feel? Are you ready to decompose into the earth? Could you say that you have used your time well on this sweet earth?

3. While still lying down, let these thoughts go, and follow the "stilling the mind and listening within" exercise on page 154.

4. When you are ready, sit up and open your journal. (A headlamp is useful here.) Write down a group of questions that you would like to ask your death. If you are grappling with a major decision or difficult situation in your life, this would be a prime candidate. But it's hard to think of any real question that would be inappropriate.

5. Pick the most important question, and journal your answer.

6. If you have strength, take on another question.

Teshuvah and the Four Winds

This ceremony refers to the teachings on the four winds in chapter 12.

Practice 43
FOUR WINDS *TESHUVAH* CEREMONY

1. Stand in the center of your Soul-O site or practice space, facing to the east. Take a deep breath, calm yourself, and listen. As in meditative walking (see practice 2), place a quarter of your attention on the breath, a quarter on the feel of your feet against the ground, and half on the world around you. Take in all that you are sensing.

2. When you are ready, ask questions appropriate to the spirit of the east that will help you to do *teshuvah.* "What needs to be renewed in my life? Am I open to the energy of birth? Do I have the necessary courage to move forward? If not, what is blocking me? Do I have balance in my life, between relationships, work, spiritual practice, exercise, leisure, and such? Is my heart balanced, that is, calm and attentive enough to let me hear others and put my ego in proper perspective? Am I open to God's ever-flowing *chesed,* loving-kindness? Do I have sufficient compassion for others?"

3. Speak or journal the responses that come to your questions.

4. Thank the spirit-energy of the east for the insights you have received.

5. Continue in each of the directions.

Sometimes I invoke the help of a grandfather tree, a rock formation, or a large cactus. I circle around my helper as I face each of the directions, exchanging *chiut* as I go along (see practices 30 and 31). I find that doing *teshuvah* in relation to a partner in the natural world is relaxing and grounding.

3. SHARE IT

Offer Your Own Prayer
My experience is that when I know where I really stand and what I really need—when I am honest with myself—prayer flows from

the heart with little effort. After completing a practice from section 2, let a prayer arise; speak your heart to God (see practice 25).

Give It to God, Give It to the Earth

Not every problem we encounter has a solution. We can pray for a difficult person to change or for a miracle cure to a parent's Alzheimer disease, but we might well find it inappropriate. Instead, we might pray for patience or strength to deal with the issue.

In addition, we might simply share our pain with God. In prayer, we can ask God to take the weight off our shoulders. And we might give our pain to God's creation, what Christian theologian Sally McFague calls God's body, to mother earth.[5] The earth, infused with God's immanent presence, the *Shechinah*, is the great recycler. Though our industrial society is pushing beyond her limits, the earth has a great capacity to turn refuse and waste into the fertilizer and soil needed to nurture new life. We can ask her to help us by sharing our pain or grief.

Practice 44
GIVE IT TO THE EARTH

1. In a comfortable position, close your eyes. Sense in your body the pain of your situation. Be with it. No doubt memories will come into your mind—of a past incident, a suffering friend, a difficult situation. Instead of letting them go as in previous meditations, sit with the image and feel it resonate in the body. Watch it with compassion for yourself and others.

2. Try to visualize the feeling. You might see a color or perhaps an image that symbolizes your pain or grief. Sit with this to make sure it feels right. Your initial image might give way to a more appropriate one.

3. When you are ready, ask the *Shechinah* if she will share this with you. (If you feel tightness or constriction, you are not ready to

give this away. Do the exercise again, either now or later.) Bend over and place your palms on the ground, and in your mind's eye, visualize your pain traveling through your palms and sinking deep into the earth. Send the image or color into the ground.

4. Thank God for the earth. Thank the *Shechinah* for her help.

5. The same process can be used with the destructive habits and attitudes that we have identified in analyzing our personalities. After feeling them in our bodies and perhaps finding an image, we can lift our hands to the sky and ask God to take them; we can place our palms on the ground and ask the earth to transform them.

14

PUTTING IT ALL TOGETHER: WILDERNESS RETREAT

I have often noticed how my own perceptions and values change when I take to the wilderness.... In wilderness, my self-consciousness and inhibitions dissolve, and I am more conscious of the whole. In the city, I hurry through my chores joylessly so I can engage in more *important* things, like work. In wilderness, I find the greatest pleasure in fixing dinner, fetching wood, and bathing in an alpine lake. In the city, I always need *something*.... In wilderness, I am content with what I have: the company of friends, the beauty of the place, the pleasure of walking. I am not aware of wanting anything.

Ellen Bernstein[1]

While the practices in *A Wild Faith* can be done as part of a general outing, there is great benefit in spending a half-day, day, or longer in wilderness retreat. Continuous Jewish wilderness practice deepens the experience of each activity. In a retreat, the whole is much greater than the sum of its parts.

PLANNING A WILDERNESS RETREAT

Most every locale, most every kind of land, most every season is a good one to do spiritual practice in wilderness. It is worth going to

166

a place where you are comfortable, preferably a place you have been before. The less you need to worry about logistics and route finding, the more you can concentrate on practice.

Getting away from crowds is useful, especially for Soul-O spot activities, but do not be discouraged if it's not possible. I generally surprise my groups by stopping for discussion and practice on a busy trail. If done in a respectful way (don't block the path), other hikers do not seem to mind. In fact, they might take an interest and ask to join you.

Always give safety concerns veto power.

Common sense is important. Do not sit on an ant farm; be aware of high season for bugs; make sure you have adequate shade and water in the summer, shelter and warm clothing in the winter. I recommend beginning your hike or retreat with a written program of practices you wish to try. You can always improvise on the spot according to the weather or the way your day is unfolding spiritually. But especially in the beginning, when you are learning how to work with the various practices, it is wise to stick with a program. Fretting about which activity to do next keeps us in our heads rather than our bodies. It diverts our attention from the natural world. Besides, there is no need to do it all today. You will have many more opportunities for practice in the future.

In general, people place too much importance on choosing this practice as opposed to that, as if the obstacle between us and God is the inability to choose the magic exercise or ritual that will turn one's spiritual life around in a flash. It might happen, but as discussed previously,[2] this is an expectation that can stifle rather than enhance spiritual practice.

ALWAYS START WITH MINDFULNESS

Many factors play into the choice of practices on a hike or retreat, such as the time available, the weather, the time of year (I like to do *teshuvah* practices before the High Holy Days), how you react to a given terrain (desert makes me more introspective; spring in the Sierra Nevada elicits praise and gratitude), which practices you did yesterday, or what you need at a given time in your life (grappling with a relationship issue, recovering from an illness, marking a major birthday).

This may seem daunting at first, but remember, when it comes to spiritual practice, less is more. You do not get points for completing a greater number of practices. Just watching the clouds while listening to the birds is a practice I can't get enough of. In beginning a spiritual practice in wilderness, it is wise to start with just a few exercises and build up.

I have refrained from writing sample practice schedules for hikes and retreats, as I fear that readers will get too attached to them. Besides, what I would suggest, say, for an observant Jew would be quite different for one who grew up with little exposure to Judaism. Instead, I have written a good deal about the dynamics of spiritual life and the specific practices in each chapter. My hope is that this will help you to make good decisions about your program of spiritual wilderness practice. In general, I find it wise to strike a balance between moving and sitting practices. Also, getting the body involved by way of body and mindfulness exercises keeps us connected to the earth and helps to maintain energy.

Choosing the right practices is mostly a matter of experience. It comes with time. When starting out, it is wise to keep expectations low and try different activities. Discover what resonates best with you.

I do have one ironclad rule: always start with mindfulness practices. In fact, if you are new to them, I highly recommend that you devote a few days of retreat to mindfulness practices alone. I cannot emphasize this enough. There is a huge difference between being in wilderness and *being* in wilderness. Plenty of people walk on a trail and hardly notice a thing. They walk in the natural world the same way they walk elsewhere—lost in thoughts and worries.

The practices in this book depend on the heightened awareness and increased concentration that come easily in wilderness to those who make a minimal effort to enter receptive mode.

MULTIDAY RETREATS

Multiday retreats can be done with friends, and this is a good way to go. Some activities can be done individually, others together. For instance, early morning and evening practice can be shared, while people strike off on their own during the day.

However, extended periods of silence and solitude are particularly valuable. They allow us to give our social selves a rest. Entirely new areas of our hearts and bodies open up to receptive awareness. It is impossible to spend significant time in silence without being profoundly affected.

The extraordinary power of a multiday solo wilderness retreat, however, makes it potentially dangerous as well. Multiday solo retreats have their own set of special needs. Preparation, entry, and reentry are not simple affairs. Extended fasting in wilderness requires some form of supervision. If problems arise, the skilled response of an experienced teacher is essential. **Therefore, I recommend multiday solo retreats in the context of a reputable organization led by a teacher you respect.** A typical program includes preparation in a group, a period of supervised solo retreat, and reentry with the group under the guidance of a teacher.

See the Resources section for organizations facilitating multiday solo retreats.

SHABBAT

Observant Jews are well familiar with retreats; they do one every week! I love celebrating Shabbat in wilderness. If I'm on a backpacking or kayak trip, I schedule Shabbat as a layover day. Nothing

teaches the power of Shabbat better than observing the day after a
week of hiking with fifty pounds on your back.

I bring two candle lanterns, wine or juice, and some special
crackers (in place of challah) for Friday night; wine and candles for
Havdalah (the ceremony marking the end of Shabbat). Usually I
find spices on the trail, but if need be, I bring them as well.

Traditionalists often bring string to put up an *eruv*, a Shabbat
boundary, so that they can carry things around the campsite.[3] They
observe the prohibitions against walking far from camp and refrain
from lighting fire. This requires some serious logistical preparation. But if Shabbat is about letting the world return to God by
refraining from manipulating the environment, then there is no
place like wilderness to experience a traditional Shabbat.

LEAVE NO TRACE

We gain so much from spiritual practice in wilderness. Let us be
the kind of people who give back to the natural world. It starts
with refraining from any activity that damages the places we visit.
If you are not familiar with "leave no trace" camping, an Internet
search will reveal appropriate resources. Any good backcountry
store will have books as well.

SAFETY

Finally, safety first.

If you are new to wilderness, know that the dangers are real.
There is no need for undue fear, but plenty of need to respect the
potential pitfalls. It is wise to go out with others who know the
ropes.

All wilderness travelers should begin their mindfulness practice at home by attending to safety. Fully acquaint yourself with
the dangers in your wilderness destination. All safety procedures
recommended by the governing bodies should be followed metic-

ulously. A wilderness first aid course pays dividends anywhere you might be.

Here are some examples of how I think about safety: On solo retreats, I don't wander; I stay in areas where people will pass nearby, or go with a partner. I carry a loud whistle; leave an itinerary and arrange for people to find me if I don't return; in deep wilderness, I carry a satellite phone. (If all goes well, it never gets turned on.) **You need to think of what's appropriate for your trip. Consult with experienced backcountry travelers if you are new to wilderness.** Multiday solo retreats should be done in the context of a group and a teacher.

If you are in therapy, consult with your therapist before practicing in wilderness for the reasons mentioned above.[4] If you are on medication prescribed by a psychiatrist, do not venture into wilderness without the consent of your caregiver. **Some people are tempted to think that in nature, they no longer need their medication.** This kind of thinking can lead to disaster!

It is not the place of this book to teach safety procedures, which vary from place to place and season to season. I can only urge you to take your safety very, very seriously.

A WILD FAITH

The experience of wilderness promises two of life's primary lessons: we find out who we are and where we belong, and we learn to live in community with other people. In the process, we have the opportunity to become proactive, to develop intimacy with each other and the land, and to participate in the process of community building.

Today, many people tend to view the biblical wilderness experience as a metaphor for the journey we must all take to confront the unknown side of our soul and gain self-knowledge. Given that almost the entire biblical story takes place in the context of the desert wandering, I am convinced that the experience of wilderness is more than a metaphor.

Ellen Bernstein[1]

If one cannot make oneself open and ownerless like this desert, one can acquire neither wisdom nor Torah.[2]
Bamidbar Rabbah 1:7

Jewish wilderness practice takes place in the natural world, but if it succeeds, the fruits of practice accompany us wherever we go.

When it works, we return to civilization with increased patience, compassion, and response-ability.

It is natural to feel a bit depressed after returning from wilderness. But we need not leave our spiritual lives behind till our next outing. We can take the excitement and energy of spiritual practice in wilderness and put it into spiritual practice at home. When I pray the traditional prayers in the city, I often remember the places I said them in wilderness, particularly prayers that mention the natural world. I purposely let my siddur, my prayer book, soak up campfire smoke so that I can smell the scent of pine or oak when I pray in the city.

This book is not about ethics, but the subject deserves mention. Spiritual practice in wilderness should lead to increased social justice activity, particularly on behalf of wilderness protection and sustainable living. If global warming and the destruction of habitat don't concern you, your practice is lacking. It's not possible to enter I-Thou without surrendering to the needs of the Thou, and by extension, all Thous. You will find outlets for political and social action on behalf of the environment in the Resources section.

A WILD FAITH

Finally, I'd like to leave you with a meditation on the nature of Jewish faith (double meaning intended).

When we enter wilderness, we begin a journey in the usual sense, and we embark on a journey of the heart as well. Wilderness inspires us; she is a great teacher.

But wild nature takes no prisoners. The love we receive is tough love. Leaving the land of permanent shelter demands our courage and fortitude. In wilderness we learn how to live fully aware of danger without anxiety. Nothing is riskier to the outdoor enthusiast than the denial of risk. Statistically, I am much more likely to die from a car accident than a grizzly attack, but I'm constantly aware of potential hazards when I'm far from a hospital. Outside the human comfort zone called civilization, I am less prone to falling into routine. The risks prod me to greater awareness.

In the city, I employ a different strategy. I avoid anxiety by "forgetting" what I know about accidents. When I drive, I'm rarely thinking about driving. Neither wilderness nor the freeways are forgiving, but in the city, I deceive myself and act otherwise.

In nature, the awareness of mortality is constant. Unlike the sanitized world of the supermarket, birth and death are encountered together in the natural world. Yet most of us see beauty, not terror. One knows without reservation that this world is sacred and good, including the mosquitoes and the lightning storms. If one learns to listen well and acts in sync with the rhythms of season and habitat—the sweet lesson of informed surrender—one feels safe, even protected, despite the risks. One can feel safer in the backcountry than in the city. An instinctive trust in oneself and in the universe is acquired. A spontaneous, naïve, organic faith arises; leaps are unnecessary.

Historically, we do not know if the Israelites actually spent forty years in the Sinai desert. But I cannot help but notice that these same wilderness attitudes are also the basis of biblical *emunah*—the Hebrew word for "trust" that came to denote faith.

Consider this: The generation that left Egypt during the Exodus is the generation of miracles. They experienced the splitting of the Reed Sea and witnessed God's revelation at Mount Sinai. Yet all but two (Joshua and Caleb) were condemned to die for lacking faith before entering the Promised Land. Who did merit entry into the Land of Israel? The generation of the wilderness. The ones who learned to overcome their anxiety and trust in the goodness of the world despite the dangers; the ones who came to believe in their own abilities to overcome the obstacles of surviving in wilderness; the ones who witnessed the daily miracle of sunrise and sunset. The parallel between wilderness trust and biblical *emunah*, it seems to me, should not be reduced to coincidence.

While not discounting the theological differences between the Hebrew Bible and the contemporary view espoused in this book, the parallels between my own *emunah*, so influenced by wilderness, and the faith of my ancestors is striking. The ancient Israelites, mostly farmers and shepherds, were intimately connected to their land. They possessed a worldview grounded in the earth and focused on this world, an animate world where spirit and material are part of the same everyday reality. Clearly seeing the dangers, they nevertheless trusted in God's justice and the goodness of God's creation. They knew their own primary role and responsibility in the determination of their fate. Yet they also knew the limits of their reach and the need for divine grace. They lived with a heightened awareness of God.

This is Judaism at its core.

A wild faith.

APPENDIX 1
BUT RABBI, IS THIS JEWISH?

R Hanina said: The Holy One's seal is truth.

Talmud *Shabbat* 55a

Truth springs up from the earth.

Psalms 85:12

When I sought teachers who connected wilderness to spiritual practice, I found very little in the Jewish world. So like many Jews in this unprecedented age of freedom and culture sharing, I took my spiritual quest outside the Jewish community. As a rabbi, I was grounded enough to be open to other traditions without feeling threatened vis-à-vis my own. But the question quickly arose: When I encounter an effective, truthful practice or ritual from another tradition, should I integrate it into my Jewish practice? Should I pursue the mindfulness practices I learned from Buddhists or exchange *chi* with a tree, as I learned from Daoists?

My own answer to these questions is a resounding yes. But I do not take such decisions lightly. The issues are serious, and the stakes are high. In this appendix, I share my thinking on the perils of adopting and adapting other people's ways into the practice of Judaism.

A COHERENT TRADITION

In considering a new spiritual practice, the problem of authenticity is inevitable. A spiritual tradition necessarily evolves in some ways and not in others. A specific set of beliefs and practices is adopted; a specific vocabulary emerges. A tradition must make choices, and this limits choices further down the line. For if innovation is too radical, or if a tradition is so open that it tries to be everything to everyone, its beliefs about the world lose coherence. Then its power to ground cultural activity and inspire creativity is lost.

Christianity, for example, has evolved in many creative and even contradictory ways. But all the various sects that call themselves Christian maintain the centrality of Jesus. Otherwise, they forfeit their claim to the inheritance of Christianity.

To take a mundane example, you can go to a basketball court with your tennis racket. No one would say that you are wrong to prefer tennis, but if you want to be on the basketball team, you have to make a choice. Either start a new kind of basketball game, as the Unitarians have done, or leave basketball, as one does in converting to another religion.

But if I hit a basketball with a tennis racket and call it basketball (Jews for Jesus), I'm not only deluding myself, I'm wrecking the sport. The game loses its coherence. The problem is not that I make a mockery of the game in the eyes of conservative defenders of the purity of the tradition. Rather, I will not score many baskets with a tennis racket in my hand. I am disempowered. I have lost the wisdom accumulated over the years by previous basketball players.

IS IT JEWISH?

So how do I decide to adopt or adapt a practice from another tradition? To my mind, the authenticity test is whether or not it can fit into the master-story of Judaism. In other words, the questions I ask of a heretofore non-Jewish spiritual practice are these: Does it conflict or cohere with the core Jewish concepts of *kedushah, tikkun,* and *b'rit* (see chapter 5)? Does it fit easily into the ongoing story of the Jewish people? Does it blend well with existing Jewish practice?

If there is an outright conflict in adopting the new practice, say taking communion in a church or bowing before a statue of the Buddha, I reject the practice, even if people I respect do it, even if I know that it embodies truth for others and potentially for me.

If the new practice does not obviously conflict with Judaism's master-story, I weigh the beliefs and values behind the practice. If they do cohere with the core concepts and rituals of Judaism, I can integrate the practice in one of two ways. Let's take Yoga as a timely example.

The first way is simple: I don't treat Yoga as a Jewish practice. I'm a Jew who does Yoga. If Yoga is my sole spiritual activity, then I am a Jew who practices another spiritual path, a Jew who does not practice Judaism. Or, I am a committed Jew who does Yoga, as it were, on the side. In this case, the beliefs and cultural norms that give structure to my spiritual life are Jewish. This is how I think of my own practice of Tai Chi and Chi Quong.

It gets more difficult if I try the second way: integrating yoga into my spiritual life as a *Jewish* practice. Can I make a Jewish Yoga? At first glance, the answer appears to be yes. If not, Judaism could not have grown and developed as it has.

No doubt, many of the forces driving the development of Judaism over the millennia resulted directly from the dynamics of Jewish spiritual practice. But any observer who has studied the societies in which Jews have lived can see their impact on Judaism. Whether it's Maimonides' reconciliation of Judaism with Aristotle in *Guide for the Perplexed* or that the notion of an afterlife is missing in Israelite culture before contact with Persian and Greek thought, Judaism has received from (and contributed to) the many cultures with which it has come into contact.

Take the Passover Seder as an example. The four cups of wine, the dipping of vegetables, the Four Questions, the *afikoman* (itself a Greek word for the last matzah eaten at the Seder) were all "borrowed" from the Greek symposium. But the more important point is that the content behind the Greek forms was recast in Jewish terms. Instead of debating philosophy or discussing the virtues of the good life, we told the story of our people's escape to freedom. In some cases, the borrowed Greek custom turned into exactly the opposite of its Greek expression. At the symposium, the *afikoman* (dessert) meant, "Start the party," while at the Seder, "No more eating!" The Greek forms, if you will, were "Judaicized." Today we think of the Passover Seder as the quintessential Jewish ritual. But at the time, these innovations were probably controversial. (Since only the rabbinic literature survived, we do not know what their opponents were thinking.)

I have treated mindfulness in a similar way. I learned it mostly from Buddhism, but I now understand it in the context of *devekut* and the core Jewish concepts of holiness, transformation, and covenant. Also, I have "Judaicized" Chi Quong practices by relating to *chiut* as part of the *shefa* rather than *chi* in the context of Daoist beliefs.

THE COST OF INNOVATION

But there is a price to be paid. In the Buddhist context, the power of mindfulness lies in its exposure of the impermanence of mind states. This important teaching is rooted in the Therevada Buddhism my teachers espoused, which in the West is more akin to psychology than religion. In contrast, Judaism emphasizes God, the Jewish people, the heart, and the soul. Buddhism, of course, has much to say about the heart, and Judaism has something to say about the mind. But if you ask where the action is, Judaism and Buddhism direct you to different places. One can find comments on impermanence in Jewish writings, but were I to speak of impermanence as a Jewish concept, I would be bringing a tennis racket to the basketball court.

Today, some Jewish innovators are keeping the forms of Tai Chi and Yoga, but attempting to ground them in Jewish language and belief, as I have done with Chi Quong by substituting *chiut* and its Jewish mystical context for *chi* and its Daoist framework. We have our work cut out for us. It's much easier to convert a wine-drinking ceremony than a Yoga pose or a Chi Quong exercise. Can Chi Quong exercises retain their potency if divorced from the Daoist beliefs that gave birth to them? Yoga can be practiced without any knowledge of the chakras, but should it? Can similar Jewish ideas, say from the Kabbalah, replace them in a Jewish Yoga? If so, would it still be Yoga?

There is only one way to figure it out.

We live in an interesting time!

APPENDIX 2

BUT RABBI, SHOULD
I TALK TO TREES?

All trees converse [*me-si-chim*] (so to speak) with one
    another;
all trees converse (so to speak) with humankind.
All trees were created for human companionship....[1]
B'reisheet Rabbah 13:2

My guess is that many readers have difficulty imagining themselves speaking directly to natural elements like streams (practice 14) or wordlessly addressing, say, a tree in order to exchange *chiut* (practice 31). In our society, talking to a river or a tree is considered crazy. I used to think that way, too. Obviously I've changed. Today, I think it is the most reasonable and sensible way to live.

DAVID ABRAM AND *THE SPELL OF THE SENSUOUS*

Have you ever wondered why our science-based, rational society teaches its toddlers through stories with speaking bears, inquisitive bees, talking sea-sponges, and wise trees? Since our science-based culture considers animals as instinct-driven, unintelligent beings and considers plants like machines, shouldn't we have outgrown that? By and large, adults in Western countries certainly have.[2]

But in other "primitive" cultures, adults have not abandoned the enchanted world of children.

I am blessed to count David Abram among my friends. His teachings are leading to paradigm-shifting sea changes in the way people understand themselves in the world. If I could, I'd ask everyone in our society to read his book, *The Spell of the Sensuous*.[3] It is stirring up diverse fields such as philosophy (in which he earned a PhD), psychology, and most important, ecology. Author Bill McKibben writes, "I walked outside when I was done [reading Abram's book] and the world was a different place."

Abram is a sleight-of-hand magician, and this turned out to be quite useful. When he lived with indigenous peoples in Bali and Nepal, his magic gave him an in with the local shamans. Abram immersed himself in native cultures and learned to see the world as they do. To indigenous peoples, every part of nature "speaks." All the inhabitants—plants and animals and rocks and streams—are animate and expressive.

A name for this worldview is "animism," a word that conjures up negative images for some. But it is simply a term for a way of experiencing the world that is common to native peoples across the planet. Every entity is not only alive; it has its own story, if we are willing to listen to language different than our own.

The animate world speaks to us moderns in the West as well. We are awestruck by a mountain range in the snow. We are inspired by the courage or persistence of an animal. We respond to the soothing sound of a river. We are shaken by the closeness of a lightning strike. We might find a particular rock to sit on that, over time, elicits our best thinking and heartfelt prayers.

In the Western world's understanding of perception, finding calm on a boulder has nothing to do with the rock. Rather, I'm projecting my feeling on the boulder. Meaning only happens in human brains. Unaware of spirit/matter, mind/body dualism, however, indigenous peoples do not have a sense of self that is limited to the insides of their bodies. The field of cognition—the place where perception is attained and meaning is made—extends far beyond the skull. They do not have the prejudice that human language is unique and superior to other means of communication. Rather, all entities speak their own languages, which interact with all the other languages in the landscape. All express themselves in ways that are intelligible to us humans. We take part in their stories; they take part in ours.

In *The Spell of the Sensuous*, Abram shows that the latest studies in human perception arrive at similar conclusions. Even in the academic world, researchers are finding that our understanding of the world is less about organizing facts in the brain and more about a conversation with the world that is carried out primarily by our bodies.[4]

With the emergence of the Gaia theory, modern science is also coming to see life on earth as a dialogue. James Lovelock introduced the idea that individual species and biospheres are part of a larger, self-regulating, intelligent organism: Gaia, the earth itself.[5] The movements of ocean currents, the exchange of gases by animals and plants, the movement of individual cells in an organism adapting to change—what is believed to be "blind" behavior driven by the laws of physics and random chance—is actually part of a very intelligent organism indeed, an organism that includes our reasoning and self-reflective minds as well.

Even an amoeba displays sentience; it reacts to the surrounding conditions in order to survive. While nothing like animal consciousness, it too makes decisions. We are making a mistake if we only associate intelligence with humanlike consciousness.

When we are open to it, the animistic world communicates with us. Without projecting humanlike consciousness on natural entities, we do find meaning in our conversations with them, which, according to Martin Buber, take place in the Between (see chapter 4). We learn about beginnings from a sunrise, stability from granite, courage from lions, compassion from chimpanzees. To recognize our place within the natural world, rather than apart from or above it, Abram coined the term "more-than-human-world" to describe the other inhabitants of the earth with whom we converse.

The fact is we cannot wean our children off speaking bears because that would greatly impoverish their development. When we stop listening to the "more-than-human-world" as adults, we impoverish our own range of meaning as well.[6]

ISN'T ANIMISM FOR PAGANS AND AGAINST JUDAISM?

This question is particularly relevant considering ancient Israelite religion. After all, an overarching theme in the Hebrew Bible is the diatribe against a paganism that based itself on animism. Nature was indeed perceived as expressive and intelligent, and so pagans worshiped natural forces as gods.[7]

But as we saw in detail in chapter 2, the biblical authors did not view nature as a machine. Rather, they experienced the natural world as animistic through and through. The land has moral agency; the sky and the earth are called upon to witness the covenant between God and the Israelites; the stars and the mountains join humans in singing the praises of God. Transcendent God appears over and over in physical modalities.

The biblical war against idolatry was not against animism per se. Rather, it was against an interpretation of animism that saw idols and mountains as objects of worship. The Hebrew Bible insists on greater transcendence in the natural world than pagans admit, a transcendence that is also responsible for ethics, a transcendence that is ultimately One. But for the Hebrews, the world was alive and expressive.

The Hebrew word that came to mean soul, *neshamah*, originally meant "breath." The word for "spirit," *ruach*, is also the word for wind. In the biblical worldview, humans and animals are directly animated by God's breath. As many commentators note, the very name for God whose pronunciation has been lost—

scholars today render it as Yahweh; it is translated as LORD in English Bibles and rendered as Adonai in gender-neutral translations—is a series of vowel sounds. Vowels, of course, are sounds of the breath. Probably because it is invisible, we lend little credence to the air. We hardly notice it. We tend to think of the space between two mountains like the space between two stars.[8] But in the biblical worldview, the tangible, sensuous air was the active home of God's involvement in the animate earth.

It is easy to see the conceptual affinity between this biblical animism and medieval Jewish mysticism, with its understanding of God's manifestation in the world as the *shefa*, the divine flow. Like the air, with the air, through the air, the earth constantly bathes in a swirl of divine energy.

Among the mystics, animism was a given. The kabbalists regularly performed what we today call magic. (The expression *abra cadabra* is Aramaic, meaning "created as spoken.") They offered incantations and prayers for healing that drew on the real (as opposed to the symbolic) power of speaking and writing to manipulate the physical world. The legend of the golem, the clay figure brought to life by writing Hebrew words on its forehead, is probably the most well-known, if exaggerated, example. While certainly not a nature cult, they assumed the animate character of the world.

The early Reform Movement in the nineteenth and twentieth centuries, with its affinity for Enlightenment rationalism, fought against the animistic side of Judaism. So did medieval and modern philosophers and rabbis, who stressed a purely spiritual conception of God. Until recently, modern Judaism was decidedly anti-mysticism. But to say that animism is pagan and therefore anti-Jewish is historically and conceptually inaccurate.

ADDRESSING THE ANIMATE EARTH
As discussed in chapter 4, Martin Buber insisted that I-Thou relation was possible with animals. And at the very beginning of *I and*

Thou, he describes a moment of genuine relation with a tree. Buber teaches us how we too might address the entities of the natural world as Thou. I added a mystical dimension to this experience based on Kabbalah (see chapter 9). Moments of I-Thou open up the floodgates of the *shefa* and bring us into bodily contact with God's *chiut* by way of the Thous of this world.

Once, Buber was asked by a friend, "Tell me: Do you believe in God?" Taken aback, he stood in silence for a moment before assuring him that he did. But later he pondered the question, asking himself, what do I really believe? Then Buber describes a moment of I-Thou in which he became a vessel for the following words that formed within him.

"If to believe in God means to be able to talk about him in the third person, then I do not believe in God. If to believe in him means to be able to talk to him, then I believe in God."[9]

Buber considered this insight crucial to his discovery of I-Thou versus I-It. This is the practical difference between relating to the world in second- rather than third-person language. In I-It, we talk *about* other beings and the world. Often this I-It position is justified, say when we analyze the natural world to make shelter, medicine, farming implements. But to enter I-Thou, we must speak *to* our potential Thou. How? By addressing the more-than-human-world with thoughts and gestures and, yes, words, that bring us into dialogue. By saying "you."

There is room for caution here, lest we repeat the errors of idolatry that our biblical ancestors rebelled against. I do not regard a volcano or an owl as a god any more than I do another person. I do not worship the natural world. Rather I say, as the yogis greet each other, *namaste*—I see the divine in you. I engage trees and mountains in dialogue in order to reveal God in I-Thou relation and to receive the *shefa*.

We Westerners have a prejudice that dialogue is an exchange of words. It seems strange that I should speak words to a tree or rock that cannot speak back, not even a bark or a purr. But Buber taught us that genuine communication is not dependent on words. I use them when communicating with a tree because I am human. Words express my heart's desire with compelling power. But just as it is natural for me to use words, it is natural for other beings to communicate in their ways. I can speak words to a tree without expecting words back.

There is no getting around it. If you were raised in a Western country, the thought of actually speaking to nature is absurd. It's no little thing to get over. My hope is that this appendix will give your intellect enough reasons to let your body and heart take a chance. I hope you'll give it a try, see how it feels, and make your own reasonable decision.

APPENDIX 3
THE NATURE OF JEWISH STUDY

> One of the things that has kept the Bible fresh, while most of ancient Near Eastern literature withered or was embalmed, is the gust of country air that hits the reader the moment he opens the book—the smell of cedar, sheep dung, sun-baked wheat and olives bruised beneath one's sandals…. In all the ancient Near East, only the Hebrew writers have dirt under their fingernails.
>
> Evan Eisenberg[1]

As we read Torah every Shabbat in synagogue, the Jewish people is likely the world's largest and longest-running book club. While Torah study is less hands-on or specific to the natural world than the other practices mentioned in *A Wild Faith*, its centrality in Jewish practice demands our attention. Torah study in the natural world is great fun, and it is often different than learning indoors.

TORAH *IN* THE NATURAL WORLD
Does reading a biblical story in the place it occurred affect one's understanding of the text?

As a newly ordained rabbi and Israeli desert guide, I led hiking retreats into the central Sinai mountains, usually with rabbis, rabbinic students, and students for the ministry. On each trip we studied chapter 19 of the First Book of Kings, for a very simple reason. The story is set at Mount Sinai.

After Elijah defeats the prophets of Ba'al in the famous contest on Mount Carmel (1 Kings 18), King Ahab's wife, Jezebel, issues a death warrant for the Hebrew prophet. Elijah flees to the desert, where he lies down to die. But God rescues him and leads him to Mount Sinai. Then God asks Elijah, "Why are you here?" a perplexing question since God miraculously brought Elijah to the mountain of revelation in the first place. Expecting to be rewarded for his service, Elijah no doubt hopes to see God on the holy mountain, something only Moses had ever done before. Instead, "Why are you here?"

Then the story gets really interesting.

> And lo, Adonai passed by. There was a great and mighty wind, splitting mountains and shattering rocks by the power of Adonai; but Adonai was not in the wind. After the wind—an earthquake; but Adonai was not in the earthquake. After the earthquake—a fire; but Adonai was not in the fire. (1 Kings 19:11–12)

To meet God, Elijah expects the dramatic smoke, thunder, and lightning that accompanied the first revelation on Sinai (Exod. 19). God dramatically appeared in fire and smoke on Mount Carmel as well. But God has a surprise for Elijah. The text explicitly mentions wind, earthquake, and fire, exactly where God is supposed to be. But three times, God is surprisingly absent.

> And after the fire—a still, small voice.[2] (1 Kings 19:12)

God is not in the storm; God is in the silence! A silence that yields a question, the very same question Elijah heard once before.

> When Elijah heard it, he wrapped his mantle about his face and went out and stood at the entrance of the cave. Then a voice addressed him: "Why are you here, Elijah?" (1 Kings 19:13)

The story raises many questions. To me, the most difficult one concerns God's rebuke of Elijah. Clearly, Elijah is guilty of some infraction. Twice God asks him an accusatory question, "Why are you here?" But what did Elijah do to deserve God's disfavor?

Traditional Jewish commentators and almost all modern biblical scholars,[3] strange bedfellows indeed, provide the same answer. God never commanded him to flee Jezebel and her soldiers. Elijah is God's prophet and therefore has God's protection. He should have stayed with the people and continued his prophetic mission. Instead, inexplicably, Elijah lost his nerve and fled Jezebel; he lost his faith in God.

But this explanation makes little sense. God did not command Elijah to challenge the prophets on Mount Carmel, either, but Elijah clearly acts in accordance with God's will. Later commentators, steeped in the theology of their own day, assume that relying on God's presumed promise to protect Elijah (no such guarantee is actually mentioned in the text) is a safer bet than fleeing the arrows of Jezebel's soldiers. In fact, no character in the Hebrew Bible places him- or herself in harm's way, thinking, "God will cause all the archers to miss."[4] And until this incident, Elijah had more nerve that any other prophet. During his career, he was fearless in the face of King Ahab's overwhelming power to kill him. So why do so many assign Elijah's sin to his sudden loss of faith? It is, I believe, because there has to be some reason for God's dissatisfaction with Elijah, and no one has an alternate explanation. Elijah must have done something wrong.

I could not think of an alternative either until I spent serious time in the central Sinai mountains. Then it occurred to me. "'Why are you here' in Sinai and not back home?" might actually be a different question: "'Why are you here' in the desert?" Perhaps God is not asking Elijah why he lost his faith. Perhaps God is asking Elijah about the quality of his faith.

Elijah expected God's dramatic, earthshaking, pyrotechnic revelation. But what did he get? What does the desert give to anyone? The "still, small voice," a revelation that can only be heard in the great gift of the desert: silence. From now on prophecy will be different. Elijah the zealot needs to learn his role model Moses's greatest virtue, his ability to listen, his humility. And so God brings him to the desert. "Why are you here?" questions Elijah's assumptions about how prophecy works, not his faith in God.[5]

NATURE IN THE STORY LINE

This interpretation of the Elijah narrative has its own problems, and you may or may not agree. But the point is this: reading a Jewish text in the natural world can open up new avenues of understanding and interpretation.

Just as it makes a difference to pray a prayer about nature *in* nature, studying Torah in the natural world provides an intriguing new perspective. This happens in various ways.

Sometimes the geography is part of the story line. Abraham expels his handmaiden, Hagar, and son, Ishmael, from his camp and sends them to the nearest settlement, Beersheva. But Hagar loses her way and needs to be rescued by God. This leads to speculation that Abraham intended for her and Ishmael to die in the desert. Would Abraham have killed his son on his own initiative?

In the mountains, it is quite difficult to keep landmarks in sight when your view is constantly narrowed by ridges or blocked by forests. But in the desert, one can usually keep uninterrupted sight of navigation markers on the horizon. That is, unless you are in an area where low-lying sand dunes surround you, where one desert wash looks like the next, and the sun is directly overhead. Even with a compass, it is almost impossible to mark a bearing and stick to it.

Ever been to Beersheva? The gentle ridges and dry riverbeds in the area form a complex labyrinth. Even a seemingly short trip that one has traveled many times before can suddenly prove a challenge, especially if one is emotionally distraught or otherwise distracted. Hagar loses her way and despairs. For the reader to make sense of the narrative, knowledge of the terrain is assumed.

Sometimes nature is a major player in a biblical story, such as God's flooding of the earth. And when God promises never to repeat the destruction, the new covenant is not limited to human beings.

> I now establish My covenant with you and your offspring to come, and with every living thing that is with you— birds, cattle, and every wild beast as well—all that have come out of the ark, every living thing on earth. I will maintain My covenant with you: never again shall all flesh be cut off by the waters of a flood. (Gen. 9:9–11)

As we saw in chapter 2, God's creation of the world often plays a key role in our understanding of God and God's relation to humans, other animals, and the planet. The same is true of the Book of Job.

Job, you might recall, protests his unjust punishment at the hands of God. In the famous speech from the whirlwind (Job 38, 39), God replies by challenging Job's assumptions. How? By giving him a tour of the natural world.[6]

Job's claim is based on what scholars call the "Deuteronomic theology," so named because it is prominent in the Book of Deuteronomy. It is the theology of reward and punishment. It claims that even what happens in wilderness, when the rain falls and where the desert replaces cultivated land, depends on whether humans fulfill or disobey the commandments. Part of God's response is to disabuse Job of that notion (italics are mine).

- Do you think you really know how the world works, Job?

> If you shout commands to the thunderclouds,
> will they rush off to do your bidding?

If you clap for the bolts of lightning,
will they come and say, "Here we are"? (38:34–35)[7]

• Do you, Job, think that I am only involved with humans?

Do *you* hunt game for the lioness
and feed her ravenous cubs,
when they crouch in their den, impatient,
or lie in ambush in the thicket? (38:39–40)

Do you tell the antelope to calve
or *ease her when she is in labor?* (39:1)

• Job, do you really think that I am unconcerned with the rest of creation?

Who cuts a path for the thunderstorm
and carves a road for the rain—
to water the desolate wasteland,
the land where no man lives;
to make the wilderness blossom
and cover the desert with grass? (38:25–27)

Indeed, Conservative theologian Robert Gordis suggested that the Book of Job provides the basis for a new Jewish environmental ethic.[8]

Finally, just getting out of the yeshiva study hall or the university library provides a fresh perspective that leads to new interpretations of Torah. In the greatest single work of Jewish mysticism, the *Zohar*, the rabbis constantly set out into the world in order to understand the meaning of the Torah they already know so well.

STUDY IT ON THE TRAIL
Like every spiritual activity in wilderness, study is aided by the relaxation and mindfulness that come with slowing down and

paying attention to the natural world. You might try contemplative study. Say a line of the text you are studying out loud. Let it resonate in the air. Sit with it before you launch into an analysis.

If you are traveling with others, you also might try the traditional method of Jewish study called *chevruta*. From the same root as *chaver* (friend), it involves study with a partner. Read the text out loud, ask as many questions as possible, and then discuss them together.

Here is a partial list of subjects and biblical texts that speak about or take place in the natural world. Reading them in wilderness might lead you to entirely different understandings.

Creation, the Garden of Eden, and the Flood—These texts at the beginning of the Torah (Gen. 1–11) deal with the relationships between God, humanity, and the natural world. If you have never studied Torah as an adult, commentaries are recommended (see Resources at the end of the book). So is a teacher. (Many synagogues, Jewish universities, and community centers offer courses on Torah study that are open to the public.) Most of the Bible, though not written as what we would call history, covers historical events that actually occurred. These sections, however, are clearly mythic. They need to be treated as master-stories rather than history or science. Unless one is ultra-Orthodox, we can accept that Judaism has evolved and changed through the centuries. With regard to women and other issues, we can refrain from judging the biblical authors from our viewpoint, three thousand years removed, and realize that we too might be considered mistaken by future generations. Without losing our own moral perspective, we might delve into the biblical text for wisdom in light of the moral and spiritual challenges we face today.

Ancestor Narratives in Genesis—Ishmael and Esau are desert men, counterparts to their farmer/shepherd brothers Isaac and

Jacob. Both are vilified in later Jewish literature as uncivilized and immoral. But in the biblical text itself, the picture is much more nuanced. After Esau threatens to kill Jacob for stealing his birthright, he matures, and on Jacob's return from Haran some twenty years later, he welcomes him with a kiss. Jacob's wrestling match with the mysterious man on the banks of the Jabbok river (Gen. 32), just before meeting Esau, is one of the pivotal texts in Jewish spirituality.

Environmental Ethics—Can the Torah contribute to environmental ethics in our time? The concepts of Sabbath, Sabbatical Year, and Jubilee in chapter 25 of Leviticus provide fertile ground.

Elijah—Running from Queen Jezebel, Elijah escapes to the desert (1 Kings 19). God leads him to Horeb, another name for Mount Sinai, the mountain of revelation. Expecting a replay of the giving of the Ten Commandments, with thunder and lightning, Elijah hears a different kind of revelation, the "still, small voice."

Psalms—Discussed in chapter 7. See practices 15 and 23.

Song of Songs—This erotic poem is understood as a metaphor for the love between God and the Jewish people. Try reading it with that special friend! It speaks about the dynamics of yearning, attraction, love, and redemption.

Job—Job is chock-full of nature metaphors that convey the ideas of the various characters. God's reply to Job out of the whirlwind in chapters 38 and 39 is an extended tour of the natural world. As I read it, wilderness is presented as a model for understanding human suffering. Following Robert Gordis (see above), many see Job as a foundation for Jewish environmental ethics.[9]

Wisdom Literature—Job and Song of Songs are part of what scholars call "Wisdom Literature," a distinct body of texts within the Bible. These books preserve traditions that often seem to contradict other parts of the canon, including the Torah. They are full of nature imagery. In particular, check out Ecclesiastes 3 and 12 and Proverbs 8.

References to the natural world, of course, can be found in every genre of Jewish text. See the Resources section for further reading on nature in Jewish sources and literature.

Finally, standard editions of the Jewish prayer book contain *Pirkei Avot*, usually translated as Wisdom (or Ethics) of the Fathers. So it's always in my backpack. It is a collection of one- or two-line gems regarding the moral life and spiritual quest, the equivalent of the Book of Proverbs for the rabbis who lived in the first centuries of the Common Era. While they do not often relate to nature,[10] I have spent many a rainstorm in my tent, snuggled in my sleeping bag, engaging this precious compendium of wisdom.

APPENDIX 4
TRADITIONAL NATURE BLESSINGS

Wilderness travel provides many opportunities to recite these blessings from Jewish tradition. For a full explanation, see chapter 8 (page 85) and practice 18 (page 90).

Upon seeing wonders of nature, including lightening, shooting stars, vast deserts, high mountains, and a sunrise:

בָּרוּךְ אַתָּה יהוה אֱלֹהֵינוּ מֶלֶךְ הָעוֹלָם, עוֹשֶׂה מַעֲשֶׂה בְרֵאשִׁית.

> Baruch atah Adonai Eloheinu Melech ha'olam, oh-seh ma'a-seih v'reisheet.
> Praised be You Adonai, our God, Sovereign of the universe, source of creation.

Upon seeing trees or creatures of striking beauty:

בָּרוּךְ אַתָּה יהוה אֱלֹהֵינוּ מֶלֶךְ הָעוֹלָם, שֶׁכָּכָה לּוֹ בְּעוֹלָמוֹ.

> Baruch atah Adonai Eloheinu Melech ha'olam, sheh-kakhah lo b'olamo.
> Praised be You Adonai, our God, Sovereign of the universe, who has such beauty in your world.

Upon hearing thunder (or upon seeing a storm):

בָּרוּךְ אַתָּה יהוה אֱלֹהֵינוּ מֶלֶךְ הָעוֹלָם, שֶׁכֹּחוֹ וּגְבוּרָתוֹ
מָלֵא עוֹלָם.

> Baruch atah Adonai Eloheinu Melech ha'olam, she-ko-cho
> u-g'vurato ma-lei olam.
>
> Praised be You Adonai, our God, Sovereign of the universe,
> whose power and might fill the whole world.

Upon seeing a rainbow:

בָּרוּךְ אַתָּה יהוה אֱלֹהֵינוּ מֶלֶךְ הָעוֹלָם, זוֹכֵר הַבְּרִית,
וְנֶאֱמָן בִּבְרִיתוֹ וְקַיָּם בְּמַאֲמָרוֹ.

> Baruch atah Adonai Eloheinu Melech ha'olam, zokheir
> ha-b'rit v'neh'ehmahn bi-v'rito v'kayam b'ma'amaro.
>
> Praised be You Adonai, our God, Sovereign of the universe,
> who remembers the covenant, is faithful to it, and keeps
> Your promise.

Upon seeing the ocean:

בָּרוּךְ אַתָּה יהוה אֱלֹהֵינוּ מֶלֶךְ הָעוֹלָם, שֶׁעָשָׂה אֶת־הַיָּם
הַגָּדוֹל.

> Baruch atah Adonai Eloheinu Melech ha'olam, sheh-asah
> et-ha-yam ha-gadol.
>
> Praised be You Adonai, our God, Sovereign of the universe,
> who has made the great sea.

Upon seeing trees blossoming for the first time in the year:

בָּרוּךְ אַתָּה יהוה אֱלֹהֵינוּ מֶלֶךְ הָעוֹלָם, שֶׁלֹּא חִסַּר
בְּעוֹלָמוֹ דָּבָר, וּבָרָא בוֹ בְּרִיּוֹת טוֹבוֹת וְאִילָנוֹת טוֹבִים
לֵהָנוֹת בָּהֶם בְּנֵי אָדָם.

> Baruch atah Adonai Eloheinu Melech ha'olam, sheh-lo chisar
> b'olamo davar, u-vara vo b'riyot tovot v'ilanot tovim
> l'hanot ba-hem b'nei adam.

Praised be You Adonai, our God, Sovereign of the universe, who has withheld nothing from the world and who has created beautiful creatures and beautiful trees for people to enjoy.

Upon smelling fragrant fruit:

בָּרוּךְ אַתָּה יהוה אֱלֹהֵינוּ מֶלֶךְ הָעוֹלָם, הַנּוֹתֵן רֵיחַ טוֹב בַּפֵּרוֹת.

Baruch atah Adonai Eloheinu Melech ha'olam, ha-notein rei-ach tov bapairot.

Praised be You Adonai, our God, Sovereign of the universe, who gives a pleasant fragrance to fruits.

Upon smelling the fragrance of trees or shrubs:

בָּרוּךְ אַתָּה יהוה אֱלֹהֵינוּ מֶלֶךְ הָעוֹלָם, בּוֹרֵא עֲצֵי בְשָׂמִים.

Baruch atah Adonai Eloheinu Melech ha'olam, borei atzei v'samim.

Praised be You Adonai, our God, Sovereign of the universe, who creates fragrant trees.

Upon smelling the fragrance of herbs or plants:

בָּרוּךְ אַתָּה יהוה אֱלֹהֵינוּ מֶלֶךְ הָעוֹלָם, בּוֹרֵא עִשְׂבֵי בְשָׂמִים.

Baruch atah Adonai Eloheinu Melech ha'olam, borei eesvei v'samim.

Praised be You Adonai, our God, Sovereign of the universe, who creates fragrant plants.

NOTES

CHAPTER 1: THE CALL OF THE WILD

1. Evan Eisenberg, "The Mountain and the Tower: Wilderness and City in the Symbols of Babylon and Israel," in *Torah of the Earth: Exploring 4,000 Years of Ecology in Jewish Thought*, vol. 1, ed. Arthur Waskow (Woodstock, VT: Jewish Lights Publishing, 2000), p. 49.

CHAPTER 2: THE STEREOTYPE OF THE "UNNATURAL" JEW

1. Ellen Bernstein, "How Wilderness Forms a Jew," in *Ecology and the Jewish Spirit: Where Nature and the Sacred Meet*, ed. Ellen Bernstein (Woodstock, VT: Jewish Lights Publishing, 1998), p. 53.

2. This label particularly hurts because it is the title of an article by a contemporary Jewish philosopher. See Steven S. Schwarzchild, "The Unnatural Jew," in *Judaism and Environmental Ethics*, ed. Martin D. Yaffe (Lanham, MD: Lexington Books, 2001), pp. 267ff.

3. These beliefs, which have filtered down to us in the popular culture, were introduced by modern scholars of the Bible. See Theodore Hiebert, *The Yahwist's Landscape: Nature and Religion in Early Israel* (New York: Oxford University Press, 1996), chap. 1.

4. Ibid., pp. 128, 152.

5. James L. Kugel, *The God of Old: Inside the Lost World of the Bible* (New York: Free Press, 2003), pp. 30–35

6. The story of Elijah and the "still, small voice" in 1 Kings 19 is the exception that proves the rule. It is shocking because for the first time, one hears God in the silence rather than the storm. See appendix 3.

7. The Israelites were the first to settle the highlands of Canaan. If you have been to Jerusalem, you know that the Judean Hills are terraced. They look like staircases. The terracing enabled the hills to be productively farmed. When archaeologists excavate these hills, the first layers of set-

tlement are Israelite. Historians speculate that the Israelites settled in the hill country because the Canaanites, with their superior ability to fashion iron, build chariots, and use them on flat ground, dominated the fertile plains of Canaan. The Israelites could not defeat them until the time of the monarchy, hundreds of years after the initial Israelite settlement.

8. These points are made throughout Hiebert, *The Yahwist's Landscape*. See the conclusion for a summary, particularly pp. 149–155.

CHAPTER 3: DO I HAVE TO BELIEVE IN GOD?

1. *Mishneh Torah*, Book of Knowledge, Basic Torah Principles 2:2, in Stein, *A Garden of Choice Fruit*, p. 65.

2. Robert, Bretall, *A Kierkegaard Anthology* (New York: Random House, 1946), pp. 120–1, 200. See also Borowitz, Eugene, *A Layman's Introduction to Religious Existentialism* (Philadelphia: The Westminster Press, 1965), pp. 37–8.

3. Rudolf Otto, *The Idea of the Holy*, trans. John W. Harvey (New York: Oxford University Press, 1958).

CHAPTER 4: FINDING GOD IN NATURE

1. Translation mine.

2. Eisenberg, "The Mountain and the Tower," p. 54.

3. Abraham Joshua Heschel, *God in Search of Man: A Philosophy of Judaism* (New York: Farrar, Straus and Cudahy, 1955), p. 46.

4. Ibid.

5. William James, *The Will to Believe and Other Essays in Popular Philosophy* (New York: Dover Publications, 1956).

6. This is the title of an anthology of the writings of Rabbi Lawrence Kushner (Woodstock, VT: Jewish Lights Publishing, 1998), who adopts this viewpoint from Heschel.

7. Heschel, *God in Search of Man*, p. 46. Italics in the original.

8. Ibid., p. 77.

9. Ibid., p. 75.

10. Ibid., p. 77. Italics in the original.

11. *Katnut* is a noun from the root *k-t-n*, which gives us the adjective for "small," *katan*. Similarly, *gadlut* is from *g-d-l*, which also yields *gadol*, or "big."

12. Lawrence Kushner, *The River of Light: Jewish Mystical Awareness* (Woodstock, VT: Jewish Lights Publishing, 2000), p. 71; *God Was in This Place & I, i Did Not know* (Woodstock, VT: Jewish Lights Publishing, 1991), p. 134.

13. For a discussion of this fascinating parallel, see Richard Elliot Friedman, *The Disappearance of God: A Divine Mystery* (London: Little, Brown, 1995), chap. 10.

14. For more on mindfulness, see chapter 6.

15. Nachman of Breslov, *Likutey Moharan, Likutey Tinyana*, sec. 63, p. 220, translation by Rabbi David Seidenberg.

16. Nachman of Breslov, trans. Shamai Kanter, in David E. Stein, *A Garden of Choice Fruit: 200 Classic Jewish Quotes on Human Beings and the Environment* (Wyncote, PA: Shomeri Adamah, 1991), p. 69.

17. See chapter 10 for more on this topic.

18. Martin Buber, "Autobiographical Fragments," in *The Philosophy of Martin Buber*, ed. Paul Arthur Schilpp and Maurice Friedman (La Salle, IL.: Open Court, 1967), pp. 25–26.

19. Maurice Friedman, *Martin Buber's Life and Work: The Early Years, 1878–1923* (Detroit: Wayne State University Press, 1988), pp. 188ff.

20. Martin Buber, *I and Thou* (Edinburgh: T & T Clark, 1937), p. 75.

21. Buber, "Autobiographical Fragments," p. 10.

22. Martin Buber, *I and Thou* (New York: Charles Scribner's Sons, 1958), pp. 7, 8.

23. Nel Noddings, *Caring: A Feminine Approach to Ethics and Moral Education*, 2nd ed. (Berkeley: University of California Press, 2003).

24. See Martin Buber, *Between Man and Man* (New York: Macmillan, 1965), p. 5, and "Autobiographical Fragments," pp. 22–26, 29–31.

25. Martin Buber, *The Way of Man According to the Teaching of Hasidism* (Secaucus, NJ: Citadel Press, 1964), chap. 6.

CHAPTER 5: A MAP OF THE HEART

1. Bernstein, "How Wilderness Forms a Jew," p. 51.

2. Babylonian Talmud, *Shabbat* 31a, in Nahum N. Glatzer, *Hillel the Elder: The Emergence of Classical Judaism* (Washington: B'nai Brith Hillel Foundations, 1959), p. 74.

3. The term "religious liberal" refers to a nonfundamentalist, not a political liberal.

4. Jewish identity is a combination of national and religious elements. Thus, it is not a contradiction for one to acquire Israeli citizenship by converting to Judaism.

5. This process is explained in detail in chapters 8 and 13.

6. See appendix 2.

CHAPTER 6: THE MINDFUL HIKER: LEARNING TO LISTEN

1. Lawrence Kushner, *Honey from the Rock* (Woodstock, VT: Jewish Lights Publishing, 2000), p. 22.

2. For this and the following practices, see Joseph Cornell, *Sharing Nature with Children, Twentieth Anniversary Edition* (Nevada City, CA: Dawn Publications, 1998), Section One, and *Sharing Nature with Children II* (Nevada City, CA: Dawn Publications, 1989), pp. 104–7.

3. Joseph Cornell, *Listening to Nature* (Nevada City, CA: Dawn Publications, 1987), pp. 33–34.

4. Ibid., p. 33.

5. New York: W. W. Norton, 1997.

CHAPTER 7: YEARNING AND GRATITUDE: OPENING THE HEART TO GOD

1. Marcia Prager, *The Path of Blessing: Experiencing the Energy and Abundance of the Divine* (Woodstock, VT: Jewish Lights Publishing, 2003), p. 15.

2. M. J. Ryan, *Attitudes of Gratitude* (New York: MJF Books, 1999), p. 6.

3. See the chapter on effort in David Cooper, *A Heart of Stillness: A Complete Guide to Learning the Art of Meditation* (Vermont: SkyLight Paths Publishing, 1999), pp. 55–64.

4. Ryan, *Attitudes of Gratitude*, p. 5.

5. Dawna Markova's image, in ibid., p. 60.

6. Here is an example. I wrote this psalm amidst the giant boulders in Joshua Tree National Park. It won't win any poetry awards, but it allowed me to articulate my yearnings at the time.

> These granite battleships,
>> always on patrol,
>> always in port.
> I look up to them as I
>> gather in the shade they give.
>
> You who peer through them,
>> above them, in them.
> You whose sight requires no eyes.
> You who sees yourself at every corner,
>> from every corner, in every corner.
>
> I would speak to You,
>> but bird song fills the air.
> I am at a disadvantage.
> Their language has no words.
> Mine cannot compare.

> Shelter me You motionless ship.
> Don't let me drift away on currents
> > that throw me around like
> > a leaf in a rapid
> but cannot move You.
>
> I reach out.
> Please God, hold on.

7. My thanks to Peter Scanlan for demonstrating the power of memorizing and offering poems in wilderness.

CHAPTER 8: SEEING THE SACRED: THE WAY OF BLESSING PART I

1. Prager, *The Path of Blessing*, p. 42.

2. The philosophically minded reader might be aware that this line of thinking can be used to argue that humans invent holiness, leading to moral and religious relativism. Since only people can speak a moral vocabulary, the product of our minds, and holiness has an ethical dimension (see chapter 5), we humans, it follows, actually invent the sacred. The supposed experience of awe and the perception of God are really ideas that people project on a morally neutral, God-less world. This is the secular side of the black-and-white, all-or-nothing kind of thinking that is usually associated with religious fundamentalists.

   I do not agree for the following reasons. The fact that perception is subjective and contentious, that moral reality and holiness are not perceived identically by all people—that there is no "absolute" morality—does not lead automatically to relativism, because perceptions can be verified by direct observation, or by the agreement of the larger community of skilled perceivers, as better or worse. I follow philosophers Hans-Georg Gadamer, Hilary Putnam, and John McDowell. I am a "perspectival realist." One can argue as to whether the best description of a sunrise is that the sun rises over the earth's horizon or that the earth revolves around the sun, but one cannot say that it is a result of the rotation of Jupiter's moons, or a thought experiment of a super-computer. We can argue over the best perspective, but not all perspectives are valid.

   Second, the claim that people project morality on a morally neutral world cannot make sense of the great "moral conversion" experiences that people have undergone in every culture over the course of human history. Let's take an example from Mark Twain. Huck Finn has been taught to regard blacks as subhumans. But after living with the runaway slave Jim, he comes to see Jim as a human being like himself. What changed Huck? If morality is projected, his "moral projection" could only result from a new moral projection. But no one taught him a new moral principle or other piece of learned information from his culture that he might project on Jim. Rather, he was changed by his perception of the world, by his I-Thou encounter with Jim. Only afterwards, as Huck thinks about his experience, does he internalize a new moral viewpoint that can then be projected on the world.

Third, the fact that some perspectives are only available to humans does not make them any less real. I cannot hear the high-frequency sounds that a dog can hear, but this does not mean that the dog is inventing what it hears. The fact that only humans can perceive moral reality does not mean that we invent it. We do not know if salmon or cheetahs perceive something akin to holiness and, if so, how it differs from our perception as beings that speak a moral vocabulary. But even if they do not perceive holiness at all, our perception of the sacred is not invalidated by human uniqueness. We have no choice but to see the world from a human vantage point, through our human bodies and language-producing minds.

CHAPTER 9: FILLING THE WORLD WITH HOLINESS: THE WAY OF BLESSING PART II

1. Martin Buber, *The Way of Response: Selections from His Writings*, ed. N. N. Glatzer (New York: Shocken Books, 1966), p. 129.

2. See chapter 4.

CHAPTER 10: HEART-SONG IN THE HEART-LAND: JEWISH PRAYER IN WILDERNESS

1. Heschel, *God in Search of Man*, pp. 48–49.

2. As an ancient language, Hebrew has a limited vocabulary. It is also an incredibly logical language. Each word is based on a root of (usually) three letters. Those complicated words you see in the prayer book are artificially long, as pronouns and prepositions are added on to nouns and verbs in Hebrew. Once you learn to isolate roots, you only need to learn a few dozen to understand the prayers. After you learn the letters and get used to reading from right to left, it's easier than it looks. Several innovative curricula, which teach you decoding skills while reading the liturgy and learning the root meanings of words, are currently on the market. (For instance, try Linda Motzkin, *Aleph Isn't Tough: An Introduction to Hebrew for Adults* [New York: UAHC Press, 2000].) If you have the chance, there is no better way to learn Hebrew than to spend time in Israel.

3. See Abraham Joshua Heschel, *The Sabbath: Its Meaning for Modern Man* (New York: Farrar, Straus and Giroux, 2005).

4. This metaphor, like all metaphors, is partial and not entirely accurate. Unlike the divine flow, the *shefa*, I can get out of, or avoid, an actual river.

5. I speak of "wilderness" in the modern sense, an area where roads and structures are illegal. The Hebrew word *midbar*, sometime translated as "wilderness," refers to semi-arid lands suitable for grazing.

6. For information and instruction on the practice of wearing *tallit* and laying *tefillin*, see Richard Siegel, Michael Strassfeld, and Sharon Strassfeld, eds., *The Jewish Catalog* (Philadelphia: Jewish Publication Society, 1973), pp. 51–63.

7. More on Rabbi Gold in chapter 11, practice 27.

8. Arthur Green, *Ehyeh: A Kabbalah for Tomorrow* (Woodstock, VT: Jewish Lights Publishing, 2004), p. 103.

9. The first version of the siddur, the Jewish prayer book, dates back to the ninth century Babylonian rabbis.

CHAPTER 11: WITH YOUR WHOLE SELF: LIVING IN YOUR BODY

1. Buber, *The Way of Response*, p. 145.

2. Lawrence A. Hoffman, *My People's Prayer Book*, vol. 1, *The Sh'ma and Its Blessings* (Woodstock, VT: Jewish Lights Publishing, 1997), p. 102.

3. Conversation with David Abram, August 10, 2006. He describes the participatory nature of perception in rich detail in *The Spell of the Sensuous* (New York: Pantheon Books, 1996), chap. 2.

4. Linda Holler, *Erotic Morality: The Role of Touch in Moral Agency* (New Brunswick, NJ: Rutgers University Press, 2002), chap. 1.

5. Abraham Joshua Heschel, for instance. See John C. Merkle, *The Genesis of Faith* (New York: Macmillan, 1985), p. 58.

6. According to Chinese medicine and my understanding of Jewish mysticism, the energy flow in your body is obstructed. Directing energy with your mental focus on the block restores the flow of *chi* or *chiut*. See practices 29–32.

7. For information and instruction on the practice of laying *tefillin*, see *The Jewish Catalog*, pp. 58–63.

8. Translation mine.

CHAPTER 12: FOUR WINDS, SEVEN DIRECTIONS

1. Here are a few of the sources for the four winds and their attributes:

> Just as the Holy One created the four directions, so too four angels surround the divine throne: Michael, Gavriel, Uriel, and Rafael.... Michael is to the right opposite the banner of Reuben, who is in the south.... Uriel is opposite Dan in the north, which is the place of

darkness. Gavriel is opposite Judah in the east. And Rafael is behind, in the west, opposite Ephraim.... And the *Shechinah* is in the west (*P'sikta Rabbati* 46:4, translation by Rabbi Jill Hammer).

There are four foundations: fire, air, water, and earth.... Fire, air, water, and earth are the primordial roots of all that is above and all that is below, and the lower and upper worlds are founded on them *(Zohar* II, 24a, translation by Rabbi Jill Hammer).

In the center of it were also the figures of four creatures. And this was their appearance: ... Each had four faces.... Each of them had a human face [at the front]; each of the four had the face of a lion on the right; each of the four had the face of an ox on the left; and each of the four had the face of an eagle [at the back] (Ezekiel 1:10).

And our earlier teachers taught that upon the flag of the camp of Reuven was the image of a human ... and the flag of Reuven was in the south. And upon the flag of Judah was the image of a lion ... and the flag of Judah was in the east. And upon the flag of Efraim was the image of a buffalo ... and the flag of the camp of Efraim was in the west. And upon the flag of Dan was the image of an eagle ... and the flag of the camp of Dan was in the north (*Sefer M'irat Eynayim, Bamidbar* [Beginning], translation by Rabbi Gershon Winkler).

2. Here I differ with Rabbi Winkler, who travels in the opposite direction—north, west, south, east—in his understanding of how the Wheel tells our life stories. See Gershon Winkler, *Magic of the Ordinary: Recovering the Shamanic in Judaism* (Berkeley, CA: North Atlantic Books, 2003), p. 55.

3. Heschel, *God in Search of Man*, p. 46.

4. Ronald Eisenberg, *The JPS Guide to Jewish Traditions* (Philadelphia: Jewish Publication Society, 2004), pp. 725–26.

5. That the horizon represents the future, and the earth the past, is a major teaching of David Abram in *The Spell of the Sensuous*, pp. 206ff., which, again, I have added to Rabbi Winkler's Medicine Wheel.

6. Associating up with transcendence and transcendence with ethics is my addition to Rabbi Winkler's work.

7. This, too, is my addition.

8. See note 5 above.

9. For information and instruction on the practice of waving the four species, see *The Jewish Catalog*, pp. 73–78.

10. The Thou, of course, may feel the same way about the need to serve us, but we do not perceive their need to serve us while in genuine relation, only our need to serve them.

11. David Abram pointed this out to me in conversation.

12. And then, only partially. The animals and their placement in the four directions derive from the mystical vision of Ezekiel's chariot (Book of Ezekiel, chap. 1). Other parts of this Jewish Medicine Wheel stem from interpretations written by rabbis living far from the Land of Israel. Sometimes they interpret a biblical text so the Israelite landscape may still come through, but certainly not from their personal experience in Israel.

CHAPTER 13: *TESHUVAH:* THE WILD HEART OF REPENTANCE

1. *Eichah Rabbah* 3:9 on Lamentations 3:43, in Stein, *A Garden of Choice Fruit,* p. 64.

2. This exercise is an element of the Death Lodge ceremony developed by the late Steven Foster. See his book, *The Book of Vision Quest,* rev. ed. (New York: Fireside, 1992), p. 36.

3. While this teaching is widespread, I received it from an important teacher of mine, Rabbi Jonathan Omer-Man.

4. Jerusalem Talmud, *Ta'anit* 4:7.

5. Sallie McFague, *The Body of God* (Minneapolis: Fortress Press, 1993).

CHAPTER 14: PUTTING IT ALL TOGETHER: WILDERNESS RETREAT

1. Bernstein, *Ecology and the Jewish Spirit,* p. 54.

2. See "Meeting the God of Small Things" in chap. 6.

3. Jewish law prohibits carrying items outside the home on Shabbat without an *eruv.*

4. See the introduction to "Practices" in chap. 13.

CHAPTER 15: A WILD FAITH

1. Bernstein, *Ecology and the Jewish Spirit,* p. 56.

2. Translation mine.

APPENDIX 2: BUT RABBI, SHOULD I TALK TO TREES?

1. In Stein, *A Garden of Choice Fruit,* p. 46.

2. With some important exceptions, such as the Middle Earth writings of J. R. R. Tolkien and the world of Harry Potter.

3. David Abram, *The Spell of the Sensuous* (New York: Pantheon Books, 1996).

4. For more on this topic, see Linda Holler, *Erotic Morality.*

5. James Lovelock, *Gaia: A New Look at Life on Earth* (New York: Oxford University Press, 2000).

6. It is impossible to present *The Spell of the Sensuous* in a short space. I urge you to read it yourself to gain a full understanding of David Abram's compelling thought.

7. There is much more to paganism, but this description fits the Hebrew Bible's characterization of it.

8. This point is made by David Abram.

9. Buber, "Autobiographical Fragments," p. 24.

APPENDIX 3: THE NATURE OF JEWISH STUDY

1. Eisenberg, *Torah of the Earth*, vol. 1, p. 51–52.

2. The JPS translation footnotes "a still, small voice"—the traditional English translation from the King James Bible. The JPS translation reads, "a soft murmuring sound."

3. A few modern commentators explain that God is asking an existential question: "How is your soul, Elijah?" But such philosophizing disrespects the text. If the author needs a dramatic story to ask that question, we need to take the story seriously and stay within its narrative parameters. Why is Elijah asked this question while he is standing on Mount Sinai, instead of back home in Israel?

4. Abraham, the direct recipient of God's promises to father the Jewish future, presents his wife, Sarah, as his sister to avoid Pharaoh's wrath (Gen. 12). Jacob, the direct recipient of God's promises, tries several ruses to avoid Esau's army when he returns to Canaan (Gen. 32). Hezekiah does not defend Jerusalem based on dogma; he repairs the city walls and prepares for war (2 Kings 18).

5. This a brief summary of my article "Elijah and the 'Still, Small Voice': A Desert Reading," *CCAR Journal*, Spring 2001.

6. Shamu Fenyvesi, "Befriending the Desert Owl," in Bernstein, *Ecology and the Jewish Spirit*, pp. 27–31.

7. Translation by Stephen Mitchell, *The Book of Job* (San Francisco: North Point Press, 1987).

8. Robert Gordis, "Ecology in the Jewish Tradition," *Midstream*, October 1995, pp. 19–23.

9. Ibid.

10. Be forewarned, however, that perhaps the most anti-nature statement in rabbinic literature is found in it: "Rabbi Jacob said, One who is walking and repeating [Jewish texts were memorized] and stops to say, 'How beautiful is this tree or this field,' is considered to have committed a capital offense" (*Pirkei Avot* 3:9). To put this statement in proper perspective, see Jeremy Benstein, "'One, Walking and Studying ...': Nature vs. Torah," in *Judaism and Environmental Ethics*, ed. Martin D. Yaffe (Lanham, MD: Lexington Books, 2001), p. 206.

RESOURCES

The following is an eclectic list of books and organizations from Rabbi Mike Comins that readers might find useful in developing a Jewish spiritual practice in wilderness. As website addresses and phone numbers change, they are not listed here. An Internet search engine will yield contact information for the organizations mentioned.

NATURE AND SPIRIT, ECO-PHILOSOPHY, ECO-THEOLOGY

ORGANIZATIONS

The Murie Center, Jackson Hole, Wyoming

BOOKS

Abram, David. *The Spell of the Sensuous*. New York: Pantheon Books, 1996.

Dillard, Annie. *Pilgrim at Tinker Creek*. New York: McGraw-Hill, 2000.

———. *Teaching a Stone to Talk*. New York: Harper & Row, 1982.

Gottlieb, Roger S., ed. *This Sacred Earth: Religion, Nature, Environment*. New York: Routledge, 2004.

Hazleton, Lesley. *Where Mountains Roar: A Personal Report From the Sinai and Negev Desert*. New York: Penguin, 1980.

Lane, Belden. *The Solace of Fierce Landscapes: Exploring Desert and Mountain Spirituality*. New York: Oxford University Press, 1998.

Lopez, Barry. *Desert Notes, River Notes*. New York: Avon Books, 1990.

McFague, Sallie. *The Body of God*. Minneapolis: Fortress Press, 1993.

———. *Super, Natural Christians*. Minneapolis: Fortress Press, 1997.

Norris, Kathleen. *Dakota: A Spiritual Geography*. Boston: Houghton Mifflin, 2001.

NATURE AND JEWISH SPIRIT

ORGANIZATIONS

TorahTrek Spiritual Wilderness Adventures

Walking Stick Foundation, Rabbi Gershon Winkler

BOOKS

Bernstein, Ellen, ed. *Ecology and the Jewish Spirit: Where Nature and the Sacred Meet.* Woodstock, VT: Jewish Lights Publishing, 2000.

_____. *The Splendor of Creation: A Biblical Ecology.* Cleveland, OH: Pilgrim, 2005.

Biers-Ariel, Matt, Deborah Newbrun, and Michal Fox Smart, eds. *Spirit in Nature: Teaching Judaism and Ecology on the Trail.* Springfield, NJ: Behrman House, 2000.

Comins, Michael. "Wilderness Spirituality." *CCAR Journal,* Winter 2006.

_____ "Elijah and the 'Still, Small Voice': A Desert Reading," *CCAR Journal,* Spring 2001.

Elon, Ari, Naomi Hyman, and Arthur Waskow, eds. *Trees, Earth, and Torah: A Tu B'Shvat Anthology.* Philadelphia: Jewish Publication Society, 2000.

Stein, David, ed. *A Garden of Choice Fruit: 200 Classic Jewish Quotes on Human Beings and the Environment.* Wyncote, PA: Shomrei Adamah, 1991.

Winkler, Gershon. *Magic of the Ordinary: Recovering the Shamanic in Judaism.* Berkeley, CA: North Atlantic Books, 2003.

JEWISH PROGRAMMING IN THE NATURAL WORLD

ORGANIZATIONS

Adventure Rabbi, Rabbi Jamie Korngold

Burning Bush Adventures, Rabbi Howard Cohen

Kosher Treks, Yedidya Fraiman

Outdoor Jewish Adventures, Josh Lake

TorahTrek Spiritual Wilderness Adventures, Rabbi Mike Comins

SOLO WILDERNESS RETREAT

(Many fine teachers are at work in this field. [For a directory, go to www.wildernessguidescouncil.org.] However, as this is an un-regulated and potentially dangerous undertaking, I am only comfortable listing the organizations whose programs I have attended myself.—MC.)

ORGANIZATIONS

Through the lens of mindfulness and Judaism:
TorahTrek Spiritual Wilderness Adventures

Through the lens of Daoism, Tibetan Buddhism, and Native American teachings:
Sacred Passage, John Milton

Through the lens of contemporary psychology:
Animus Valley Institute, Bill Plotkin et al.

BOOKS

Foster, Steven, and Meredith Little, *The Book of the Vision Quest.* New York: Fireside, 1992.

Linn, Denise. *Quest.* New York: Ballantine, 1999.

WILDERNESS SKILLS AND SAFETY

ORGANIZATIONS

Backpacker Magazine (Online and print)

The Mountaineers Books

The National Outdoor Leadership School

Outward Bound

The Sierra Club

Wilderness Medical Associates

BOOKS

Berger, Karen. *Trailside Guide: Hiking and Backpacking.* New York: W. W. Norton & Company, 2003.

Fleming, June. *Staying Found: The Complete Map and Compass Handbook,* 3rd ed. Seattle: Mountaineers Books, 2001.

Hart, John. *Walking Softly in the Wilderness: The Sierra Club Guide to Backpacking.* Berkeley: University of California Press, 2005.

Harvey, Mark. *The National Outdoor Leadership School Wilderness Guide: The Classic Handbook, Revised and Updated.* New York: Fireside, 1999.

Kals, W. S. and Clyde Soles. *Land Navigation Handbook: The Sierra Club Guide to Map, Compass & GPS.* Berkeley: University of California Press, 2005.

Morrissey, Jim. *Wilderness Medical Associates Field Guide.* Portland, ME: Wilderness Medical Associates, 2000.

Schimelpfenig, Tod. *NOLS Wilderness Medicine,* 4th ed. Mechanicsburg, PA: Stackpole Books, 2006.

JUDAISM AND ECOLOGY

ORGANIZATIONS

The Adamah Fellowship at Isabella Freedman Jewish Retreat Center

The Coalition on the Environment and Jewish Life (COEJL)

My Jewish Learning (for study materials on this and most any Jewish subject)

The Teva Learning Center

BOOKS

Benstein, Jeremy. *The Way Into Judaism and the Environment.* Woodstock, VT: Jewish Lights Publishing, 2006.

Eisenberg, Evan. *The Ecology of Eden.* New York: Alfred A. Knopf, 1998.

Hareuveni, Nogah. *Desert and Shepherd in Our Biblical Heritage.* Kiryat Ono, Israel: Neot Kedumim, 1991.

Hiebert, Theodore. *The Yahwist's Landscape: Nature and Religion in Early Israel.* New York: Oxford University Press, 1996.

Tirosh-Samuelson, Hava, ed. *Judaism and Ecology: Created World and Revealed World.* Cambridge, MA: Harvard Divinity School, 2002.

Waskow, Arthur, ed. *Torah of the Earth: Exploring 4,000 Years of Ecology in Jewish Thought.* 2 vols. Woodstock, VT: Jewish Lights Publishing, 2000.

Yaffe, Martin D., ed. *Judaism and Environmental Ethics: A Reader.* Lanham, MD: Lexington Books, 2001.

ENVIRONMENTAL ACTION

ORGANIZATIONS

Earth Justice

The Natural Resources Defense Council

The Rainforest Action Network

The Sierra Club

The Wilderness Society

JEWISH ENVIRONMENTAL ACTION

ORGANIZATIONS

The Coalition on the Environment and Jewish Life (COEJL)

Hazon, Nigel Savage

The Heschel Center (Israel), Jeremy Benstein, Eilon Schwartz

The Israel Union for Environmental Defense, Alon Tal

The Shalom Center, Rabbi Arthur Waskow

SPIRITUAL PRACTICE

BOOKS

Boorstein, Sylvia. *Don't Just Do Something, Sit There.* San Francisco: HarperSanFrancisco, 1996.

———. *Pay Attention, for Goodness' Sake: Practicing the Perfections of the Heart—The Buddhist Path of Kindness.* New York: Ballantine Books, 2002.

David Cooper. *A Heart of Stillness: A Complete Guide to Learning the Art of Meditation.* Woodstock, VT: SkyLight Paths Publishing, 1999.

Kornfield, Jack. *A Path with Heart.* New York: Bantam Books, 1993.

Orloff, Judith. *Positive Energy.* New York: Harmony Books, 2004.

SPIRITUAL PRACTICE IN NATURE

BOOKS

Cornell, Joseph. *Listening to Nature.* Nevada City, CA: Dawn Publications, 1987.

———. *Sharing Nature with Children, Twentieth Anniversary Edition.* Nevada City, CA: Dawn Publications, 1998.

———. *Sharing Nature with Children II.* Nevada City, CA: Dawn Publications, 1989.

Hinchman, Hannah. *A Trail through Leaves.* New York: W. W. Norton, 1997.

Lionberger, John. *Renewal in the Wilderness: A Spiritual Guide to Connecting with God in the Natural World.* Woodstock, VT: SkyLight Paths Publishing, 2007.

Plotkin, Bill. *Soulcraft.* Novato, CA: New World Library, 2003.

JEWISH SPIRITUAL PRACTICE

ORGANIZATIONS

The Aleph Alliance for Jewish Renewal

C-Deep, Rabbi Shefa Gold

The Elat Chayyim Center for Jewish Spirituality

The Institute for Jewish Spirituality

Metivta, A Center for Contemplative Judaism

The National Havurah Committee

NeoHasid, Rabbi David Seidenberg

The Union for Reform Judaism, Department of Lifelong Jewish Learning

BOOKS

Boorstein, Sylvia. *That's Funny, You Don't Look Buddhist: On Being a Faithful Jew and a Passionate Buddhist.* San Francisco: HarperSanFrancisco, 1997.

Schachter-Shalomi, Zalman. *Jewish with Feeling: A Guide to Meaningful Jewish Practice.* Woodstock, VT: Jewish Lights Publishing, 2013.

Prayer

Prager, Marcia. *The Path of Blessing: Experiencing the Energy and Abundance of the Divine.* Woodstock, VT: Jewish Lights Publishing, 2003.

Levy, Naomi. *Talking to God.* New York: Doubleday, 2002.

Hoffman, Lawrence A. *The Way Into Jewish Prayer.* Woodstock, VT: Jewish Lights Publishing, 2000.

Comins, Mike. *Making Prayer Real: Leading Jewish Spiritual Voices on Why Prayer Is Difficult and What to Do about It.* Woodstock, VT: Jewish Lights Publishing, 2010.

Schachter-Shalomi, Zalman, and Joel Segel. *Davening: A Guide to Meaningful Jewish Prayer.* Woodstock, VT: Jewish Lights Publishing, 2012.

Chant

C-Deep, Rabbi Shefa Gold (www.rabbishefagold.com)

Gold, Shefa. *The Magic of Hebrew Chant: Healing the Spirit, Transforming the Mind, Deepening Love.* Woodstock, VT: Jewish Lights Publishing, 2013.

Hernández, Ana. *The Sacred Art of Chant: Preparing to Practice.* Woodstock, VT: SkyLight Paths Publishing, 2005.

Meditation

Davis, Avram, ed. *Meditation from the Heart of Judaism: Today's Teachers Share Their Practices, Techniques, and Faith.* Woodstock, VT: Jewish Lights Publishing, 1999.

Cooper, David A. *The Handbook of Jewish Meditation Practices: A Guide for Enriching the Sabbath and Other Days of Your Life.* Woodstock, VT: Jewish Lights Publishing, 2000.

Gefen, Nan Fink. *Discovering Jewish Meditation: Instruction and Guidance for Learning an Ancient Spiritual Practice*, 2nd ed. Woodstock, VT: Jewish Lights Publishing, 2011.

JEWISH THEOLOGY

BOOKS

Gillman, Neil. *Believing and Its Tensions: A Personal Conversation about God, Torah, Suffering and Death in Jewish Thought.* Woodstock, VT: Jewish Lights Publishing, 2013.

————. *Traces of God: Seeing God in Torah, History and Everyday Life.* Woodstock, VT: Jewish Lights Publishing, 2006.

Cosgrove, Elliot J., ed. *Jewish Theology in Our Time: A New Generation Explores the Foundations and Future of Jewish Belief.* Woodstock, VT: Jewish Lights Publishing, 2010.

Artson, Bradley Shavit. *God of Becoming and Relationship: The Dynamic Nature of Process Theology.* Woodstock, VT: Jewish Lights Publishing, 2013.

Abraham Joshua Heschel

Heschel, Abraham Joshua. *God in Search of Man: A Philosophy of Judaism.* Northvale, NJ: Jason Aronson, 1987.

————. *The Sabbath.* New York: Farrar, Strauss and Giroux, 2005.

Kaplan, Edward K. *Holiness in Words: Abraham Joshua Heschel's Poetics of Piety.* Albany: State University of New York Press, 1996.

Merkle, John C. *The Genesis of Faith.* New York: Macmillan, 1985.

Martin Buber

Buber, Martin. *Between Man and Man.* Translated by Ronald Gregor-Smith. New York: Routledge, 2002.

————. *I and Thou.* Translated by Walter Kaufman. New York: Scribner, 1970.

————. *The Way of Man: According to Hasidic Teaching.* Translated by Bernard H. Mehlman and Dr. Gabriel E. Padawer. Woodstock, VT: Jewish Lights Publishing, 2012.

————. *The Way of Response: Martin Buber, Selections from His Writings.* Edited and translated by N. N. Glatzer. New York: Shocken Books, 1966.

Vermes, Pamela. *Buber on God and the Perfect Man.* London: Littman Library of Jewish Civilization, 1994.

JEWISH MYSTICISM

Cooper, David. *God Is a Verb*. New York: Riverhead Books, 1997.

Green, Arthur. *Ehyeh: A Kabbalah for Tomorrow*. Woodstock, VT: Jewish Lights Publishing, 2004.

Kushner, Lawrence. *God Was in This Place & I, i Did Not Know*. Woodstock, VT: Jewish Lights Publishing, 1991.

———. *The River of Light: Jewish Mystical Awareness*. Woodstock, VT: Jewish Lights Publishing, 2000.

Ouaknin, Marc-Alain. *Mysteries of the Kabbalah*. New York: Abbeville Press, 2000.

POETRY

Barks, Coleman. *The Essential Rumi*. San Francisco: Harper, 1995.

Bly, Robert, ed. *The Soul Is Here for Its Own Joy*. New York: MJF Books, 1997.

Norris, Gunilla Brodde. *Sharing Silence, Becoming Bread, Journeying in Place*. New York: Quality Paperback Book Club, 1996.

Oliver, Mary. *House of Light*. Boston: Beacon Press, 1990.

Rilke, Rainer Maria. *Rilke's Book of Hours: Love Poems to God*. Translated by Anita Barrows and Joanna Macy. New York: Riverhead Books, 2005.

Whyte, David. *Fire in the Earth*. Langley, WA: Many Rivers Press, 2002.

HEBREW COURSES

Motzkin, Linda. *Aleph Isn't Tough: An Introduction to Hebrew for Adults*. New York: UAHC Press, 2000.

TORAH COMMENTARIES

Etz Hayim: Torah and Commentary. Philadelphia: Jewish Publication Society, 2004.

Friedman, Richard Elliot. *Commentary on the Torah*. San Francisco: HarperSanFrancisco, 2001.

The JPS Torah Commentary. 5 vols. Philadelphia: Jewish Publication Society, 1989.

The Torah: A Modern Commentary. Rev. ed. New York: URJ Press, 2005.

Zornberg, Avivah Gottlieb. *Genesis: The Beginning of Desire*. Philadelphia: Jewish Publication Society, 1995.

INDEX TO PRACTICES

JOIN THE CONVERSATION AT
www.awildfaith.com

Dear Reader,

I would love to hear your feedback regarding the practices in *A Wild Faith*—how they affect your spiritual life and your wilderness experience. Do you have ideas for new practices or refinements for the practices in this book? Do you have advice for your fellow spiritual seekers in wilderness based on your own wilderness practices?

Your input will help us all to further develop Jewish spiritual practice in the natural world. I would love to incorporate your wisdom into my teaching, my training of retreat leaders, and future editions of *A Wild Faith*.

Shalom and Good Walking,
Rabbi Mike Comins

Log onto www.awildfaith.com and:

- Share your experience of spiritual practice in wilderness.

- Offer suggestions to help others practice Judaism in wilderness.

- Keep abreast of *TorahTrek* programs and Rabbi Comins's teaching schedule.

- Learn new practices as they are developed.

- Share photographs and stories from your wilderness journeys.

- Post on the bulletin board and find other like-minded people for spiritual practice in wilderness.

About Jewish Lights

People of all faiths and backgrounds yearn for books that attract, engage, educate, and spiritually inspire.

Our principal goal is to stimulate thought and help all people learn about who the Jewish People are, where they come from, and what the future can be made to hold. While people of our diverse Jewish heritage are the primary audience, our books speak to people in the Christian world as well and will broaden their understanding of Judaism and the roots of their own faith.

We bring to you authors who are at the forefront of spiritual thought and experience. While each has something different to say, they all say it in a voice that you can hear.

Our books are designed to welcome you and then to engage, stimulate, and inspire. We judge our success not only by whether or not our books are beautiful and commercially successful, but by whether or not they make a difference in your life.

For your information and convenience, at the back of this book we have provided a list of other Jewish Lights books you might find interesting and useful. They cover all the categories of your life:

Bar/Bat Mitzvah	Life Cycle
Bible Study / Midrash	Meditation
Children's Books	Men's Interest
Congregation Resources	Parenting
Current Events / History	Prayer / Ritual / Sacred Practice
Ecology / Environment	Social Justice
Fiction: Mystery, Science Fiction	Spirituality
Grief / Healing	Theology / Philosophy
Holidays / Holy Days	Travel
Inspiration	Twelve Steps
Kabbalah / Mysticism / Enneagram	Women's Interest

www.ingramcontent.com/pod-product-compliance
Lightning Source LLC
Jackson TN
JSHW020018141224
75386JS00025B/581